Harris Museum and Art Gallery, Preston.

Shire County Gu

LANCASHIRE

John Champness

Shire Publications Ltd

CONTENTS

Printed in Great Britain by C. I. Thomas & Sons (Haverfordwest) Ltd, Press Buildings, Merlins Bridge, Haverfordwest, Dyfed.

British Library Cataloguing in Publication Data: Champness, John. Lancashire. — (Shire county guide; 28). 1. Lancashire — Visitors' guide. I. Title. 914. 27'604858. ISBN 0-85263-984-8.

Cover: *St George's Quay and the Priory Church, Lancaster.*

ACKNOWLEDGEMENTS
The author acknowledges with gratitude the help, advice and encouragement which he has received from friends and colleagues in the County Planning Department of Lancashire County Council, and especially from Derek Taylor, Don McKay and Geoff Morries in the Environmental Planning Unit, and from Rob Wilsher, Christine Jones and Pat Donoghue in the Tourism Unit.
    The photographs were taken by the author except for those on pages 30, 38, 47, 48, 51, 54, 60 and 61, which were taken by Cadbury Lamb.

Glasson Dock.

Fairsnape Fell and Parlick on the western edge of Bowland.

1
An overview of Lancashire

There is no place in Lancashire from which one can see the whole county, but there is no way in which it is easier to see most of Lancashire in the course of a short journey than by driving over Longridge Fell. Drive up from Longridge to Jeffrey Hill, turn right over the summit of the ridge, turn left at the New Drop Inn and pass along the southern flank to Kemple End.

You will see first of all the Fylde Plain north of Preston, and then to the east the flat-topped massif of the Forest of Bowland, with the valleys of the Loud and Hodder in front of it; then, from the summit of the fell the lower parts of the Ribble valley, including Preston, will come into view, in front of the West Lancashire Plain, which is backed by the sea on the west and by a succession of hills on the south — from Parbold Hill, on the right, past Winter Hill (with the television masts) to the Rossendale Fells. Lastly, as you approach Kemple End, you will catch sight of the middle reaches of the Ribble, behind which rises the long ridge of high ground which culminates in the summit of Lancashire's great hill, Pendle.

On occasion one can see the mountains of Snowdonia and the Lakeland fells, but on any reasonably fine day the view will encompass in a 5 mile (8 km) drive two-thirds of the county's area. Two important features which you will, however, miss are Lancaster and the Lune valley, and the belt of industrial towns which stretch westwards from Blackburn to Colne behind the long ridges of the Pendle Hill massif.

In a way, therefore, you might find the view, despite all its grandeur, somewhat deceptive; where are the dark satanic mills? It is not unfair, though, to reply that most people's mental image of Lancashire is now out-of-date, for, since the re-drawing of its boundaries in 1974, the new county of Lancashire is a predominantly rural area. Three-quarters or more of its 1,380,000 inhabitants live in urban areas, but the major industrial towns are tightly concentrated and hemmed in by hills.

Even within its traditional boundaries, Lancashire is a relatively young county and seems to have begun its independent administrative existence almost by chance. A separate entry for 'Lancastria' first occurs in the royal tax returns for the year 1181-2, but only — apparently — 'because there was no place for it in Northumberland'.

Before the Norman Conquest, what we call Lancashire was a mixed area, inhabited — to judge from place-names — by a mixture of people, the descendants of the Brigantes and their prehistoric predecessors whom the Romans conquered, veterans from the Roman army itself, Anglo-Saxons who had arrived from the east through the Aire Gap and

3

Norsemen who had come by sea from Ireland, Scotland and the Isle of Man. The area was a no man's land, claimed for equally good historical reasons by both the King of England and the King of Scots. After the Conquest it was part of England's north-west frontier.

The area south of the Ribble was given into the safe keeping of one of William the Conqueror's kinsmen, Roger of Poitou, who seems to have established himself at Penwortham, where a castle mound still stands by the parish church. However, when King William Rufus captured Carlisle in 1092, the border with Scotland was firmly fixed and 'Lancashire' became merely the second line of defence. Nevertheless, to strengthen further this second line, Roger was given both the northern half of Lancashire and the Furness area, because in those days the main road from Scotland ran around the Cumbrian coast and across the sands of Morecambe Bay. Roger therefore moved the administrative centre of his estates to Lancaster, to a site already fortified by the Romans, from which an invading Scots army would be clearly visible. His estates were called the Honour of Lancaster, and in due course its name was transferred to the county — for Lancashire is but Lancaster-shire.

It is sometimes called the County Palatine, because in 1351 Edward III rewarded Henry, the fourth Earl of Lancaster, for his military success during the war with the French by raising him to the dignity of Duke — only the second one to be created — and by giving him 'palatinate' powers for life, that is the powers of the royal palace, which included the right to establish his own chancery, or civil service, and also his own courts to try civil and criminal cases (and thereby make money from legal fees). Within the boundaries of the county, the Duke was virtually a king.

The first Duke died in 1361, but his son-in-law, John of Gaunt, persuaded Edward III, whose fourth son he was, to grant him in 1362 the title of Duke and in 1377 full palatinate powers; and in 1390 he sold his support to Richard II in return for the right for him and his male heirs to enjoy both ducal rank and palatinate powers for ever. When John of Gaunt died, his son, Henry, was in temporary exile, so Richard confiscated his estates and exiled him for life — a high-handed action which alarmed many of his other barons. In reaction, Henry invaded Yorkshire with a handful of men in July 1399 and, by swearing an oath at Doncaster that he sought nothing more than his rights and a reform of the government, won the allegiance of the major northern barons. He then persuaded Richard to negotiate but took him prisoner at Flint and transferred him to the Tower of London.

Despite his oath, he then staged a *coup d'état* in September and was acknowledged to be King Henry IV by a compliant Parliament. By February 1400 the rightful King Richard was dead in Henry's castle at Pontefract. Since that time the lands of the Duchy have belonged to the monarch, though they have been administered separately, and the Queen in consequence is the Duke of Lancaster — a fact which prompts Lancastrians, unmindful of the treacheries at the beginning of the story, to make their proud and distinctive reply to the Loyal Toast: 'The Queen, the Duke of Lancaster'.

In spite of its close connections with the royal family, Lancashire in the middle ages was a relatively poor county. Tax returns show this, while a good indication of this poverty is its small number of medieval church towers: there are no more than 35 in an area of about 1160 square miles (3100 sq km), and all but two or three of these are late medieval. Chapter 4 will show that half of the better churches in the county date from after the Reformation.

The view from Longridge also reveals the reason for this poverty: the narrowness of the belt of land which could then be cultivated, between the mosses (or fens) and ill drained claylands to the west and the acid soils on the eastern uplands — above 500 feet (150 metres) or so. Most of these uplands were useless for agriculture and were therefore designated as royal hunting forests, commemorated to this day by such place-names as the Forests of Bowland, Pendle and Rossendale. They are still vast tracts of land with little agricultural potential and, as chapter 2 will show, offer great scope to those who want to 'get away from it all' and enjoy solitude and fine scenery.

Although the Duke of Lancaster has been the King of England since 1399, Lancashire has played only a small part in the political life of the kingdom. No major battle was ever fought on its soil, not even in the Wars of the Roses, unless one counts the battle of Preston in August 1648, when, after capturing the bridge over the Ribble, Oliver Cromwell's army in a series of skirmishes along the road to Warrington effectively destroyed the army of Scots who were Charles I's last hope of winning the Civil War.

Lancashire's poverty has made it a backwater for most of its existence — and therefore conservative in its attitudes. This may explain the strength of the gentry's allegiance to the traditional Catholic faith after the Reformation, especially in the Ribble valley and the plains of the south-west and of the Fylde — but it must be added that the monasteries in the north-west were popular because of their vitality and charitable generosity. The excommunication of Elizabeth I by the Pope in 1570 placed gentlemen's consciences in a dilemma, and the fines for non-attendance at church put

Hoghton Tower.

a strain on their pockets. Thomas Hoghton of Hoghton Tower had already gone into exile in 1569 and was to support the English college at Douai (founded by William Allen of Rossall), where the sons of English Catholic gentry could be educated; John Towneley of Towneley Hall went to prison in several places and for several years; others like Richard Shireburne of Stonyhurst were more conformist: he went to church but blocked his ears with wax! Most had private chapels where they and their tenants could occasionally hear mass, but priests saying the mass were automatically guilty of high treason and several paid the ultimate penalty.

Lancashire remained the most Catholic of all the English counties during the sixteenth and seventeenth centuries, and religious convictions underlay political sympathies for the King, rather than Parliament, in the Civil War, and even — though with diminishing effect — in the two Jacobite rebellions of 1715 and 1745.

Religious tensions have virtually died out but the Whit Walks, which still continue in some places, were until the early twentieth century occasions of less than friendly rivalry, as congregations from the various churches and chapels processed their way around their town.

Lancashire Catholicism was of much greater significance than Lancashire witchcraft, but the latter — romanticised — has caught the

popular imagination and is now used to promote tourism in the north-eastern parts of the county. It is a fact that on 18th March 1612, just outside Colne, a Halifax pedlar called John Law refused to give some pins to a beggar, Alison Device, that she was angry with him and that almost at once he had a stroke. It is also true that nine women, found guilty of murder by witchcraft, were hanged at Lancaster on 20th August of that year. To modern sceptics the fact that there was a trial at all seems largely due to the obsessive interest of one magistrate, Roger Nowell of Read Hall, while much of the evidence on which the women were found guilty seems to be little more than a desire to find fame or not to lose face, even at the price' of death, and, out of spite and vindictiveness due to family quarrels, to bring about the death of others.

It is doubtful that witchcraft, which involved alleged pacts with the Devil to cause people harm and death, was significantly more prevalent around the great hill of Pendle than elsewhere in England, but during much of the seventeenth century belief in the power of magic charms to heal, and to harm, was widespread, though condemned by Protestant clergymen. A balanced account of the 'Pendle witches' can be found in the Pendle Heritage Centre (see chapter 6), and the doyen of Lancashire historians, J. J. Bagley, believes that a shippon full of cattle would be a more appropriate symbol for Jacobean Pendle than

CHAPTER 1

a witches' sabbath — but people still flock to Pendle Hill at Hallowe'en!

The belief in fairies and spirits like 'boggarts' survived among country folk into the late nineteenth century — long enough for it to be exploited until modern times in the sentimental outpourings of a few local writers.

Lancashire came to the forefront of national life during the eighteenth and nineteenth centuries, when it was one of the cradles of the industrial revolution. Even the present county, which has lost most of the industrial centres of the traditional county, contains many visible reminders of that period and chapter 7 introduces the most important sites. They include working textile mills, new towns and villages of Victorian times, but also memorials of the new forms of transport, without which industry could never have thrived and developed. The newest of these is the motorway, and the first one in Britain was the Preston bypass, which was opened in 1958 and is now part of the M6.

The worst slums, fortunately, disappeared long ago and survive only in old photographs and the horrendous descriptions in the reports of royal commissions. Some of the smaller mill villages, however, still have decent cottages built by enlightened millowners for at least the skilled members of their workforces, and most towns have mechanics' institutes, which provided a form of self-help education for skilled working men. A few towns, like Preston and Lancaster, have parks laid out during the 'cotton famine' caused by the American Civil War, and others have galleries or museums endowed by local businessmen (see chapter 6). In Lancaster Sir Thomas Storey paid for the Storey Institute in 1887, and 22 years later Lord Ashton gave the town its new town hall.

Most of the more famous Lancastrians lived in the eighteenth and nineteenth centuries. Perhaps the most famous of all is John of Gaunt, the 'time-honoured Lancaster' of Shakespeare's play, *Richard II*, but he probably spent no more than a fortnight in Lancaster in the whole of his life. The earlier Earls of Derby, members of the Stanley family, lived in the county at Lathom House, and the two sieges of the house in 1644 and 1645 are among the most stirring episodes of the Civil War. James Hargreaves invented the 'spinning jenny' in Stanhill in 1764, and five years later in Preston Richard Arkwright developed an improved spinning machine, later called the 'water-frame'. Preston was also the birthplace in 1832 of the movement for 'tee-total' abstinence, begun by Joseph Livesey and Dicky Turner, whose stammer was the origin of the word.

In the field of the arts, Richard Gillow, the celebrated furniture designer, was born in 1732 and worked all his life at Lancaster. Henry Tate was born at Chorley in 1819 and, having made a fortune in the sugar-refining industry, founded the gallery in London which now bears his name. The Brontë sisters were educated in Cowan Bridge, and Mrs Gaskell wrote several of her novels at Silverdale. Among entertainers of modern times have been the comedian Eric Morecambe, who adopted the name of his home town as his surname, the singer Kathleen Ferrier, who came from Blackburn, and, a generation further back, Wallace Hartley from Nelson, who was the leader of the band which continued to play as the *Titanic* sank beneath them.

The development of the textile industries stimulated the growth of coal mining and also of the engineering industry in its many forms. Coal mining has declined almost to extinction, and the cotton industry is now a shadow of its former self, but engineering continues to develop its traditions. Buses and trucks are still made at Leyland, jet engines at Barnoldswick, and fighter aircraft at the British Aerospace factory at Warton near Preston. Electricity is generated from two nuclear power stations at Heysham, though this is a source of anxiety rather than pride for many people. Every town has an industrial estate, and what is now the Prestige Company's factory on Colne Road, Burnley, was the first ever factory built by a local authority — in 1937 — to encourage new industry in a town whose staple industry was in decline. This same spirit of entrepreneurial self-help can best be seen in the pioneering activities of Lancashire Enterprises Limited. This economic development company was set up by the county council in 1982 to encourage new industry with advice, capital and cheap floor space, often in converted mills: in partnership with financial institutions and authorities at local, national and European level, it has done so with considerable and growing success.

Many old industrial sites, especially those related to coal mining, have now been reclaimed and where there were once slag heaps and subsidence 'flashes' there are now rolling hills given back to agriculture and trees, playing fields and boating lakes. Something of a green and pleasant land has been re-created among the few remaining dark satanic mills.

A stream in the Forest of Bowland.

2
Coast and countryside

There can be few counties which offer to the visitor a more varied series of landscapes than does Lancashire. An hour's drive can take one from saltmarshes lapped by sea water warmed by the North Atlantic Drift, across drained fenland which provides some of England's finest arable soils, through the pastoral Ribble valley dotted with limestone outcrops, to the millstone grit moorlands of the Pennines and their outliers, where the climate can be at times sub-arctic.

The short drive over Longridge Fell, mentioned at the beginning of chapter 1, reveals the major contrast between the lowland western and the upland eastern halves of the county: in the west there are landscapes which in geological terms are very recent — say, 20,000 years old — and are formed from a thick blanket of boulder clay spread by retreating ice sheets over the underlying rocks; in the east, however, the landscapes reflect fairly closely the forms of the rocks beneath, which were laid down between 300 and 350 million years ago and later corrugated into ridges and troughs by major movements in the earth's always mobile crust, perhaps 280 million years ago.

The outline of the Lancashire landscape has been drawn by nature, but the details have been filled in and often greatly altered by the will of men. Nowhere is this more clearly seen than around the coasts: during the nineteenth and twentieth centuries along the Fylde erosion of the land by the sea has been arrested and the advance of the sand-dunes checked, while the Ribble estuary and Morecambe Bay have been made considerably less extensive. Half of the coastline of the county has been changed beyond recognition as, generation by generation, tidal embankments have been built to reclaim saltmarsh from the sea, most recently on the edge of Cockerham and Pilling marshes.

The most striking landscapes are, as one would expect, in the uplands of the county, and Areas of Outstanding Natural Beauty have been designated around Arnside and Silverdale, and also in the Forest of Bowland (which extends eastwards to include Pendle Hill). The purpose of this action is to protect the relatively unspoilt character of these areas by strict development control. In addition, the county council, with neighbouring local authorities, has developed a local plan for the West Pennine Moors area — the western half of the Rossendale massif — again to strike a balance between improved access for the public and the protection of the features which they come to enjoy.

Arnside-Silverdale Area of Outstanding Natural Beauty

The Arnside-Silverdale AONB straddles the county boundary with Cumbria to encompass the most attractive part of the Lancashire coastline, the peninsula of low limestone cliffs and saltmarshes which juts out between the estuaries of the Keer and the Kent, and the wooded hills which form its hinterland.

Apart from Warton Crag and Arnside Knott, with their open summits and extensive views across the bay to Bowland and to the Lakeland fells respectively, the AONB contains for the most part small-scale enclosed landscapes, with fields of pale-green grass fringed with silvery walls of limestone, or rocky hillsides often clad in deciduous scrub or woodland, once coppiced to provide fuel for the local iron industry before the growth of Barrow-in-Furness in the mid nineteenth century. The woods are perhaps the most attractive feature of the area, and at Eaves Wood, which climbs up the hill to the north of Silverdale, the National Trust has waymarked a nature trail which enables one to appreciate the variety of old-established and more recently planted trees.

The underlying rocks are frequently revealed as limestone pavements, deeply fissured because the stone is easily dissolved by rain water; these vertical cracks then become the home of lime-loving plants like hart's tongue fern, dropwort and lily of the valley.

This is an area where it is easy to see the results of the many changes in sea level which occurred during the ice ages: when the level dropped, rivers scoured out deep valleys which were filled first with silt and then with peat, when the sea rose and fell again. Much of the resulting fenland has been drained, but the drainage of Leighton Moss was stopped during the First World War, and the area has reverted to the traditional landscape of meres surrounded by reed-beds, where the Royal Society for the Protection of Birds has established a bird sanctuary. A little to the north, Hawes Water is one of the only two natural lakes in the county (the other being Martin Mere, near Burscough).

This is an area for pleasant rambles in the countryside or around the coast, but Arnside is often the departure point for the fascinating guided walks across Morecambe Bay (see below).

Forest of Bowland Area of Outstanding Natural Beauty

Between the peaceful valley of the Lune, an area whose picturesque beauty has been appreciated since Georgian times, and the almost equally beautiful valley of the Ribble and its parallel tributaries, the Loud and the Hodder, the great massif of the Forest of Bowland rears up behind its undulating fringe of lower hills. In many ways, with its flattish summit plateaux blanketed in peat, it is similar to the Pennines and Rossendale, but its rocks are slightly older and more varied and give a greater variety to the landscape with occasional outcrops of limestone and the associated ash-trees, and more evident remains of foldings where strata which were once horizontal are now nearly vertical. There are no significant coal seams in the Forest of Bowland, and so it has never been subjected to industry nor had its packhorse trails widened into trunk roads. It is therefore still the most unspoilt area of Lancashire: only one road crosses it — the winding, narrow, bumpy road through the pass called the Trough of Bowland; the rest is accessible only to walkers.

The county council has negotiated access agreements with landowners (and published an explanatory leaflet) so that it is possible to ramble on the slopes of Clougha (near Lancaster) and Fairsnape (near Chipping) and, if adequately equipped to cope with sudden changes in the weather, to walk over the tops from the Langden Brook to Oakenclough and then, perhaps, down well wooded Grizedale; or from Quernmore to the valley of the Tarnbrook Wyre and back again; or, most strenuously and most splendidly, from Slaidburn along the line of the old Roman road up Croasdale Brook and then off the bare fells and down the valley of the Roeburn, with its picturesque hanging woods, to Wray, and then to Hornby in the Lune valley.

On its southern edge Bowland drops sharply to the linked valleys of the Loud and the Hodder, dotted with the occasional outcropping knoll of limestone, lying roughly between the villages of Chipping and Slaidburn (see chapter 8). Upstream of Slaidburn is Stocks Reservoir, opened in 1932 to provide water for the people of Blackpool but now more generally accessible, and especially to anglers. Further up the Hodder valley the road climbs up over the bleak moors to the summit of Cross of Greet, from where there are superb views northward and eastward to the great limestone mountains of the Craven area; then it drops gently down to High Bentham and ultimately to the Lune valley.

The AONB continues beyond the wide sweep of the Ribble valley, to embrace the great whale-backed mass of Pendle Hill, which stretches in two parallel ridges from Blackburn to Colne. The easy way up is the long, slow walk from the Nick of Pendle, with good views on both sides to the rural valley of the Ribble or the urbanised valley of Pendle Water with

Crossing the sands of Morecambe Bay.

the Pennines behind it. A quicker way up, which involves a steep climb, is from Barley.

West Pennine Moors

Between the Lancashire towns of Accrington, Blackburn and Chorley and the Greater Manchester towns of Bolton and Bury stretch the 90 square miles (230 sq km) of the West Pennine Moors, where the local authorities have combined to manage the relatively unspoilt countryside in such a way that visitors may enjoy it without harming the interests of those who live and work there. There are country parks in the area at the Jumbles Reservoir and at Rivington (see below).

The area is in form a shallow dome of uncultivable moorlands, based on hard gritstones and seamed with the long straight lines of dirty drystone walls. The dome is gashed by two north-south valleys which have long been used by roads: between Edgworth and Blackburn the road follows a Roman alignment. In most of the lower parts of the valleys reservoirs have been built to supply water power to mills or drinking water to the towns in the surrounding lowlands; most of them are now used for fishing, and on the Belmont, Delph and Jumbles reservoirs one may also sail. Depending on the weather, the high moors can be bleak and inhospitable, or they can possess an austere dignity, even a grandeur. Virtually everywhere is only a couple of miles from a road, and a network of ancient trackways between old farmsteads — some no longer in use because of the harsh climate and poor acidic soils — makes this a walker's paradise in good weather.

Outdoor activities

The county council publishes a series of illustrated leaflets, under the general heading of 'Lancashire's Great Outdoors', which are available free of charge from all tourist information centres (see chapter 9). The one entitled *Walking* gives more detailed information than this book can and should be used in conjunction with this chapter.

COUNTRY PARKS

Beacon Country Park. 1 mile east of Skelmersdale, off the minor road from Upholland to Dalton.

Here some 300 acres (120 ha) of open countryside rise to a ridge (which culminates in Ashurst Beacon), from where there are extensive views both over west Lancashire and eastward over Wigan to the West Pennine Moors.

Beacon Fell Country Park. 5 miles south-east of Garstang.

This well signposted country park offers 185 acres (75 ha) of countryside and conifer plantations, with a visitors' information centre just to the east at Carwags, a network of footpaths, an orienteering course and extensive views over the Fylde and the Bowland Fells.

Cuerden Valley Country Park. 4 miles south of Preston, between Bamber Bridge and Whittle-le-Woods, and accessible from B5256 (east of M6, exit 28).

This large tract of open farmland lies along the river Lostock, with picnic sites, circular paths and bridleways, and a lake.

Jumbles Country Park. 3 miles north of Bolton and accessible from B6391 ¼ mile south of Turton Tower.

This country park takes advantage of the pleasantly wooded setting of the Jumbles Reservoir, with picnic areas, fishing facilities, an information centre and a 1½ mile nature trail around the reservoir.

Rivington Country Park. Just south of Rivington, on the eastern bank of the Rivington Lower Reservoir.

These 400 acres (160 ha) of meadow and rural parkland were laid out in the early years of the twentieth century. There are cafes and an information centre at Great House Barn.

Witton Country Park. 2 miles south-west of Blackburn, just to the north of A674.

Within the 224 acres (90 ha) of the Witton Park estate are a visitors' centre, cafe and exhibition gallery in the former stable block, sports facilities and a variety of trails and walks.

Wycoller Country Park. 2½ miles east of Colne, and signposted off B6250.

Here there are over 500 acres (200 ha) of varied moorland landscape, with walks in and around the historic village, with its visitors' centre, cafe and craft shop, old houses and quaint bridges.

WALKS, PATHS AND CYCLEWAYS
The Brontë Way

This 9 mile (15 km) route comprises a strenuous hill walk over the Pennine watershed from Wycoller Dean to Haworth in West Yorkshire, passing features associated with the novels of the Brontë sisters. A leaflet is available.

The Lancashire Cycleway

Two cycleways — North and South Lancashire — cover over 300 miles (500 km) of varied Lancashire scenery from the Fylde and west Lancashire to the hills of Bowland, east Lancashire and the West Pennine Moors. Passing through many villages, the two cycleways meet at Whalley. Leaflets are available.

Morecambe Bay Guided Walks

10 mile (15 km) walks across the sands of Morecambe Bay are organised between May and September by the official guide, Mr Cedric Robinson of Guide's Farm, Cark, near Grange-over-Sands, Cumbria (telephone 04484 2165). The panoramic views from sea level are outstandingly beautiful, but on no account should this walk be undertaken without the guide, as the sands can be extremely dangerous, even deadly.

The Pendle Way

This 54 mile (90 km) walk covers the scenery and settlements of the Pendle district, including the 'Witches' Country'.

The Ribble Way

This 70 mile (110 km) walk follows the course of the Ribble from Longton, west of Preston, to its source at Ribblehead in North Yorkshire. A guidebook is available.

River Lune Footpaths: Lancaster to Glasson, and Lancaster to Bull Beck.

A 6 mile (10 km) path and cycleway runs along the track bed of the former Lancaster to Glasson Dock railway, with pleasant countryside and extensive views over the estuary and its wildfowl. There is a picnic site at Conder Green.

Another 6 mile (10 km) path, in part a cycleway, runs along the track bed of part of the former railway line between Lancaster and Wennington; it follows the riverside and crosses both viaducts at the Crook o' Lune, where it links with the North Lancashire Cycleway (see above). There is a picnic site at Bull Beck.

The Rossendale Way

This 45 mile (70 km) route winds around the valleys and moorland of Rossendale. A pack of leaflets and a guidebook are available.

OUTDOOR SPORTS
Leisure Lakes, near Mere Brow. 1 mile south-west of Mere Brow (on the A565 Preston-Southport road).

Set within 90 acres (40 ha) of open parkland are two large lakes with sandy beaches and facilities for fishing, sailing and windsurfing; there are also a nature trail and a lakeside restaurant.

Pine Lake Resort, near Carnforth. 1 mile north of Carnforth, by M6 exit 35A.

This inland holiday complex with a hotel and chalets has a 70 acre (30 ha) lake where one can practise sailing, windsurfing and water-skiing.

Ski Rossendale, Haslingden Old Road, Rawtenstall.

This is the largest dry ski centre in England, open all the year round, with a licensed cafe, a ski school with qualified instructors, a nursery slope, an intermediate slope and a main slope which is 200 yards (180 metres) long. All slopes have ski-tows and are floodlit.

NATURE RESERVES ETC
HAPPA Rest Home, Shores Hey, off Halifax Road, Briercliffe. 500 yards east of the hamlet

of Lane Bottom (3 miles north-east of Burnley).

The sanctuary is run by the Horses and Ponies Protection Association for horses, ponies and donkeys which have been rescued from cruelty and neglect.

Healey Dell Nature Reserve. 1 mile south of Whitworth, off B6377.

This local nature reserve has a visitors' centre and a nature trail, which passes through a moorland clough, with very varied plant and animal life, and across a 112 foot (34 metre) high viaduct over the river Spodden.

Leighton Moss Nature Reserve. Royal Society for the Protection of Birds. Off the minor road ¼ mile east of Silverdale station.

This is a nationally important wetland reserve for waders and wildfowl. It has an exhibition centre and shop, and also a nature trail and hides accessible from a public foot-path.

Martin Mere: Wildfowl Trust, Martin Mere, Burscough, Ormskirk L40 0TA. Telephone: 0704 895181. 2½ miles north-west of Burscough Bridge.

Martin Mere is one of the six reserves established by Sir Peter Scott's Wildfowl Trust; its 350 acres (130 ha) are the home of 1500 birds, ranging from colourful ducks, geese and swans to elegant flamingos, and a temporary resting place each year for thousands more. There are nine hides overlooking different habitats — lake, marsh and meadowland — and a shop, a coffee shop and picnic facilities.

Valiants Shire World, Lancaster Road, Out Rawcliffe. 1½ miles north of Great Eccleston, over the Wyre at Cartford Bridge and on the road to Pilling.

This is the largest Shire horse centre in Britain, with over a hundred horses on an 80 acre (32 ha) farm. There is also a display of old carriages and farm implements and a large indoor riding centre.

GOOD VIEWPOINTS

The following are all accessible by car. They are listed with the number of the Ordnance Survey 'Landranger' map on which they will be found, together with a six-figure grid reference.

Anglezarke: Leicester Mill Quarry (OS 109: SD 622162).
Ashurst Beacon (OS 108: SD 500079).
Beacon Fell (OS 102: SD 568428).
Darwen Tower (OS 103: SD 678215).
Jeffrey Hill (OS 102: SD 639401).
Jubilee Tower (OS 102: SD 542573).
Nick of Pendle (OS 103: SD 772385).
Padiham Heights (OS 103: SD 786367).
Parbold Hill (OS 108: SD 505106).
Rivington Pike (OS 109: SD 643138).

Fairsnape Fell from Beacon Fell.

3
Ancient monuments

Lancashire was settled in prehistoric times, but early remains, other than indistinct earthworks, are few and far between, though most museums contain a few artefacts in their collections. During the Roman era the area of the county was in the military zone, where pre-Roman life went on undisturbed — though stimulated economically by the presence of the army — on the understanding that it did not disturb the Roman peace. The main visible remains are therefore the alignments of roads and the remnants of forts at Lancaster and Ribchester, together with a few dozen altars, memorials and milestones now found in local museums. In the middle ages, and indeed up to the time of the industrial revolution, the area was poorer than most parts of England, so there are only a very few castles, abbeys and other structures to recall to us the life of the wealthier classes in medieval times. The better churches and houses of that age feature in chapters 4 and 5 respectively.

PREHISTORIC AND ROMAN
Castercliff, Nelson (OS 103: SD 834383). A mile or so east of Nelson, a little north of the golf course.

Built on high ground, Castercliff is the best preserved prehistoric site in the county, a roughly square hillfort, protected on all sides except the south-east by steep natural slopes. Its history is unknown. The first 6-inch Ordnance Survey map, surveyed in 1844, shows three rings of ramparts, but since then most of the stones which strengthened the outer face of the earthen banks have been removed, and only a double bank and ditch now remain. The site is also pockmarked by small-scale eighteenth-century coalpits; each is indicated by a ring of waste material, dug out and not properly shovelled back when the pit became too dangerous to work.

Cow Ark: Roman Road.
From the top of Jeffrey Hill on Longridge Fell part of the route of the Roman road which ran between Manchester and Carlisle is clearly visible, running north-east towards Newton. In the middle distance it appears as a straight line of hedgerows marking field boundaries and aligned on Pen-y-ghent, but on occasion it is possible to walk along the actual route: the most accessible stretch is marked on the Ordnance Survey sheet 103 between points SD 658437 and 667451.

Lancaster: Bath-house and Wery Wall.
The earthworks visible in Vicarage Field to the north-west of the Priory Church appear to be medieval rather than Roman, though the hilltop site above a ford over the Lune is known to have been occupied since the foundation of a Roman fort by Agricola in AD 79. This fort was extended and rebuilt several times during the 350 years of the Roman occupation, and the foundations and actual roadway of the eastern gateway of the stone-built second-century fort were found near the site of the Judges' Lodging; the main street of the civilian settlement outside the fort underlies Church Street. The only clearly visible relic of the Roman presence in Lancaster is what is thought to have been a bath-house, which was discovered in 1973 and can be reached by turning to the right off Vicarage Lane (from the Priory to St George's Quay). The foundations of three or four rooms can be seen, including the stone pillars which supported a floor to allow the hot gases from a furnace to heat the room above. This building was destroyed in about AD 330 in order to cut a ditch to run outside the latest Roman fort; its profile can be clearly seen breaking through the bath-house walls. The rugged chunk of rubble masonry beyond the railings — the Wery Wall — is thought to have been part of the base of a corner tower of this fourth-century fort.

Ribchester: Fort and Bath-house.
Ribchester is the only Roman settlement in Lancashire whose Latin name (*Bremetennacum*) is known. The fort was built by Agricola in AD 79 to guard a ford over the Ribble, while he was pioneering the upland route between Manchester and Carlisle; part of this road can be seen near Cow Ark (see above). Early in the next century a cavalry regiment was stationed there to control the district. The river has washed away the south-eastern third of the fort, but the ditch around the rest is more or less complete and can be seen beyond St Wilfrid's church. Behind the White Bull pub on Church Street the excavated foundations of part of a second-century bath-house can be seen, and the small museum (see chapter 6) by the entrance to the churchyard is worth visiting.

MEDIEVAL
Clitheroe Castle.
Standing on a rocky outcrop of limestone about 100 feet (30 metres) above the valley of the river Ribble, the keep of Clitheroe Castle is a prominent landmark in the town, with good views over the surrounding countryside. It was probably built in 1186 by Robert de Lacy to protect the administrative centre of his

Clitheroe Castle.

Halton Cross.

vast estate, the Honour of Clitheroe. It stood within a protective wall, but no other medieval buildings remain on the site. The former Steward's House now contains the Castle Museum (see chapter 6).

The keep is said to be the smallest in England, since the rooms are only about 20 feet (6 metres) square. The entrance to it now passes through what was once a window into what was a cellar; the original entrance was on the right on the floor above and was reached by an external staircase of wood, which no longer survives. In the adjacent corner turret is a spiral staircase which rises to the second floor and to the battlements.

After being held for six weeks by Royalist troops in 1644, the castle was slighted in 1649 on the orders of the Commonwealth government. The keep was restored in 1848 with smooth-faced limestone blocks, which contrast markedly with the original walling.

Halton: Castle Hill and Cross.

Now a commuter suburb just north-east of Lancaster with several fine late seventeenth-century farmhouses, Halton was before 1066 the headquarters of an extensive estate, which included Lancaster and was owned by Tostig,

the Earl of Northumberland. This probably explains why the conical mound of a motte and bailey castle rises just to the east of the church on a natural spur of land; it must have been built by the new Norman landowner to ensure that he remained in possession.

Another reminder of pre-conquest life stands in the churchyard. This is an early eleventh-century cross, whose shaft is carved not merely with obviously Christian scenes like the Crucifixion but also with scenes from the old Norse saga of Sigurd, which also tells of the triumph of good over evil.

Heysham: St Patrick's Chapel.

Perched on the low sandstone cliffs just beyond the churchyard in Heysham village stand the roofless walls of a tiny rectangular building which is called St Patrick's Chapel. It owes its name to the unlikely tradition that the saint himself built it as a thank-offering after being saved from shipwreck on the rocks below, but it dates more probably from the ninth century.

To the west of the chapel are six body-shaped graves hewn out of the rock, with a separately cut socket at the head of each for a cross. They originally had stone covers and were used for the burial of important people. To the south of the chapel was a pre-conquest graveyard where the remains of about eighty bodies were discovered during excavations in the 1970s.

Hornby: Castle Stede and Loyne Bridge (OS 97: SD 583598).

The Castle Stede at Hornby, with its prominent mound and extensive ramparts, is the best example of a Norman motte and bailey castle in Lancashire, and its original purpose — to control the crossing point of the Lune between Hornby and Gressingham — is clear. The attractive stone bridge was built in 1684 to replace a ford. The motte and bailey were superseded later in the middle ages by the stone-built Hornby Castle, but the permanent military significance of this site is shown by the concrete pillbox, which was placed there in 1939.

Lancaster Castle and Shire Hall.

The name Lancaster implies the existence of a Roman fortress, and the Normans established themselves here soon after the conquest for the same reasons as the Romans a thousand years before. The site controls the lowest crossing point of the Lune, at a place where the river is still navigable by sea-going vessels, and also commands fine views over the sands of Morecambe Bay — the normal medieval route from Scotland.

A castle was built here by Roger of Poitou, the area's first Norman lord, but, despite local legends, it was not the large three-storey keep, almost unseen in the middle of the Prison, because this is typical of the mid twelfth century.

Just as Roger cannot have built the keep, so John of Gaunt did not build the great gatehouse which bears his name and a statue of him. It is nevertheless one of the finest examples in England of a late medieval gatehouse with gates, portcullis and machicolations. The oldest part is the gateway itself, which may well have been built by King John. The heraldry on the shields on either side of John of Gaunt's statue, which was not placed there until 1822, proves that the gatehouse was built not by him but by his son, who usurped the throne in 1399 and became Henry IV.

The part of the castle which visitors see now (the entrance is on the other side, opposite the Priory Church) was largely built at the end of the eighteenth century to the designs of Thomas Harrison. It comprises two courtrooms: the very beautiful vaulted Shire Hall, which contains a magnificent display of shields of kings, sheriffs and constables of the castle since the time of Richard I, and the Crown Court, where one can still see the iron 'M' with which convicted malefactors were branded on the hand until 1811. Other grim relics of prison life in the past are in Hadrian's Tower, in the dungeons, where one can be plunged into absolute darkness, and in the Drop Room, where until 1865 prisoners were prepared for their public execution. The scaffold was erected opposite the churchyard, at what is still called Hanging Corner, so that hundreds of people could enjoy the spectacle.

Salley Abbey, Sawley. English Heritage. 3½ miles north of Clitheroe, off A59.

Founded in 1148, this was the first Cistercian Abbey in Lancashire but little now remains of it. After the abbey's dissolution in 1537 most of the cut stone in the buildings was removed, so only foundations and a few ragged walls survive. The arch which stands by the road was built up from medieval fragments in the middle of the nineteenth century.

The ruins show the austerity of the original church and then how, in the fifteenth century, the nave of that church was drastically shortened while the choir was extended to the east. This was because the lay brothers, who had originally done most of the manual work of the community, had been replaced by servants who were not monks, and because the choir monks who sang the seven daily services had increased in number.

Warton Old Rectory. English Heritage. 1 mile north of Carnforth on a minor road off A6.

The Old Rectory stands on the other side of the road from St Oswald's parish church, behind the present vicarage. Though a roofless shell, it clearly displays the standard layout of a fourteenth-century manor house. To the left as one enters, there are three identical doorways, of which the central one led through a corridor to the outside kitchen and the others led to storerooms for food and drink. They had above them a room with a fireplace, where the owner and his family could have had some privacy.

The tall room on the right was the hall, a communal living room for the family and servants of the lord of the manor and also the administrative headquarters of the manor.

Whalley Abbey, Whalley. 6 miles north-east of Blackburn on a minor road off A59.

Whalley Abbey was the last monastery to be built in Lancashire, but the monastic community — Cistercians, as at Salley Abbey — had been founded in 1172 at Stanlow in Cheshire. Having received the Pope's permission to move to north-east Lancashire, where they owned land already, twenty monks arrived in Whalley in 1296. The foundation stone of their abbey church was laid in 1330 and the first mass was sung in the completed choir in 1380. The high altar is marked by a large block of

The gatehouse of Lancaster Castle.   *Five doorways at the Old Rectory at Warton.*

stone, but virtually nothing remains of the church except foundations, though the fifteenth-century canopied stalls in which the monks stood to sing the services can now be seen in the parish church (see chapter 4).

The accommodation of the monks is relatively well preserved in parts. Immediately south of the church is the cloister, where the attractive doorway in the east wall marks the entry to the chapter house. Through this doorway is the long undercroft, above which was the monks' dormitory, with the impressive remains of the latrines at the south end. On the south wall of the cloister is a shallow recess for the trough where the monks washed their hands before going into the refectory for their two daily meals.

The west side of the cloister is cut off by a wall, behind which stands a fine two-storey building. This was completed in 1415 to contain a storehouse on the ground floor and the lay brothers' dormitory on the first floor. The extensive building to the east of the

cloister is what remains of the abbot's house but cannot be visited. It had a separate entrance — the imposing late fifteenth-century gatehouse off Church Street, which is the present entrance to the abbey ruins. The original entrance to the abbey itself was through the gaunt fourteenth-century gatehouse (by the railway viaduct) which belongs to English Heritage.

Towneley Hall (see chapter 5) contains among its treasures two priests' vestments from Whalley Abbey, which are virtually unique in England. These were made in the early fifteenth century from Italian cloth of gold, on which were sewn decorative bands of what was called *opus anglicanum* (or English work). These are embroideries worked with exquisite delicacy by English craftsmen using coloured silks and silver threads to represent scenes from biblical stories, like the Birth of Christ and the Adoration of the Three Wise Men. Such work was exported all over Europe in medieval times.

4
Churches and chapels

Most of the finest of the county's churches have been built since the late eighteenth century and include as many built for Methodists and Roman Catholics as for Anglicans. The cathedrals at Blackburn and Lancaster and the churches of Kirkham and Pleasington are among the best, but one could name a dozen more of equal quality which are not open to the public. Many of them were the work of what one might call a nineteenth-century dynasty of Lancashire architects: Thomas Rickman, his pupil Edmund Sharpe, who trained Edward Paley, who took Hubert Austin into partnership. Most Victorian churches lack the fittings and furnishings which add to the attractiveness of older churches, but the contribution of their towers and spires to the townscapes of Lancashire is often considerable.

Blackburn Cathedral: St Mary.

The finest early nineteenth-century church in the county is St Mary's at Blackburn, which stands discreetly in a large churchyard and is

Blackburn Cathedral.

now the Anglican cathedral. It was repaired after a fire in 1831 to the designs of John Palmer and Thomas Rickman, with a tall west tower, tall three-light windows in the aisles, and a very spacious, well lit interior. The gilded cresting below the clerestory windows and the many-ribbed vault with its richly carved bosses at the intersections of the ribs are especially attractive.

After the creation of the Anglican diocese in 1926, the old parish church was expanded eastwards to make it a more worthy setting for the Bishop's throne and the accompanying ceremonial. The Second World War intervened, however, before the work could be finished, and so the church was completed on a less sumptuous scale. Instead of the massive central tower originally planned, a glazed octagon of reinforced concrete was raised above the crossing, and it casts a golden glow over the high altar. Externally, the octagon and its spire form an attractive composition with the western tower. Internally, the cathedral has a number of striking modern fittings, notably the spiky metalwork crown over the high altar and the figure of Christ above the west door.

Bolton-by-Bowland: St Peter and St Paul.

Standing between the two greens in the attractive village of Bolton-by-Bowland, the church was built in the mid fifteenth century. It is typical of many churches in the Craven area by being fairly long and somewhat low, but its tower is one of the finest in the county and is unusual in having bell openings in both stages above the roof.

The interior is somewhat disappointing, but it contains a good set of seventeenth-century pews, a fine early sixteenth-century font with a concave-sided octagonal bowl decorated with the coats of arms of local gentry families, and an incised fifteenth-century grave cover of considerable human interest. It commemorates Sir Ralph Pudsay, his three wives and their children, all of whom are represented in three rows of small figures beneath the much taller figures of their parents. In the lower folds of her gown each wife has the Roman numeral indicating the number of children she bore: six, two and seventeen.

Churchtown: St Helen.

Situated at the end of the village of Churchtown, St Helen's, which was the parish church for Garstang until St Thomas's chapel was built there in 1770, claims to be the 'Cathedral of the Fylde'. The church has a complicated building history and dates back at least to the

16

St Helen's church, Churchtown.

St Cuthbert's church, Halsall.

beginning of the thirteenth century, when the two arcades of the nave were built, probably within a few years of each other. To the south of the chancel arch is an opening in which the underside of a spiral staircase can be seen. Before the Reformation, this would have led to the rood-loft, a gallery carrying statues of Christ on the cross, flanked by St Mary and St John. The roof of the chancel is dated 1620; the roof of the nave looks similar and was probably built at the same time.

From the outside the church looks largely fifteenth-century, and this is because the tower, which is unusual in having a little stone spire to crown the top of its staircase turret, dates from that time, as do most of the windows in the aisles. The finest aisle windows are those of the Lady Chapel, which was built out to the south of the south aisle; it has a good roof dated 1529 and some very interesting seventeenth-century wall paintings with biblical texts set in scroll-like frames, now unique in the county.

Great Mitton: All Hallows.

This church has the finest collection of tombs in the county. It dates from the late thirteenth century, and the prettiest feature of that date is the triple seat for the priest and his

servers in the chancel. The bottom half of the chancel screen is late medieval, with the figures in the doors representing the Annunciation; it probably came from Salley Abbey.

The finest feature of the church is the Shireburne Chapel, which projects to the north and is approached from the chancel through a pretty Elizabethan screen. It was probably built originally as a chantry chapel but was rebuilt in 1594 as the family burial chapel by Sir Richard Shireburne, who was also building Stonyhurst. The monuments range in date from the damaged effigy of a fifteenth-century knight to fine mid eighteenth-century wall tablets.

The grandest is the alabaster memorial to Sir Richard and his wife, Maud, which stands more or less in the centre. Their effigies lie stiffly on their backs in the medieval manner, he in armour, she in a rich gown whose petticoats show that the memorial was once painted. Beneath them on the tomb-chest are figures of their children and the coats of arms of the families with whom the Shireburnes had intermarried.

On the wall between the windows stands another alabaster monument, to another Richard, who died in 1628, and his wife, Anne — the next generation. They face each other,

17

St Peter's church, Heysham, with the ruins of St Patrick's Chapel in the background.

kneeling at a prayer desk, set within an arch flanked by two pairs of Corinthian columns carrying a full achievement of arms. Below the couple, to the right, there are kneeling figures of their surviving sons and daughters and, to the left, their three children who had already died.

The next three monuments were old-fashioned when they were carved in the 1690s for Lady Isabel Shireburne by William Stanton of London, one of the most famous sculptors of his time. The recumbent effigies represent Lady Isabel's father-in-law and husband, who died in 1669 and 1689 respectively, and Lady Isabel herself, who died in 1693. The tall monument against the west wall is in the grand manner with Corinthian pilasters supporting a segmental pediment; it commemorates Richard Shireburne, who died, aged nine, in 1702 after eating poisonous berries.

Halsall: St Cuthbert.

This is the earliest church in the county which is not merely pleasing or archaeologically interesting but aesthetically impressive as well. Its distinctive spire which rises from a square base through an octagonal bell-chamber, was probably designed around 1400 and is similar to two others at the nearby churches of Ormskirk and Aughton. Projecting from the tower and half hiding the porch is the former grammar school, founded by Edward Halsall in 1593. It was originally a two-storey building but was altered to only one in the early nineteenth century.

The church itself is older than the tower.

The nave was built about 1325 with a four-bay arcade on either side. The chancel may well have been built at the same time as the nave but was largely rebuilt in the later fourteenth century. It has older features inside, like the vestry door, with its splendid display of tracery, and a canopied recess on the north side which contains the alabaster effigy of a priest. Another fine tomb, on the other side of the chancel bears the effigies of Sir Henry Halsall, who died in 1523, and his wife, Margaret Stanley.

The chancel, like the nave, is rather dark and looks finer from the outside. Here one can see how well integrated the design is, with its tall three-light windows between deep buttresses which finish in pinnacles, its pair of stair turrets at the west end and, on the ridge, the bellcote for the sanctus bell, which was rung at important moments during the mass.

Heysham: St Peter.

St Peter's at Heysham is more quaint than beautiful, with its huddle of low roofs and double bellcote at the west end. When first built, perhaps in the late tenth century, it must have been less than half its present size — a simple rectangular building, fairly tall and narrow. The chancel was lengthened in the early fourteenth century, as the curving tracery in the east window and in the now unglazed window between the chancel and the south aisle shows. The south aisle of the nave was added perhaps 150 years later and then extended halfway along the chancel in the seventeenth century, when the south porch was also built and the chancel arch widened. The north aisle is dated to 1864.

St Peter's is famous for its two pre-conquest stones — a 'hogback' tombstone in the south aisle and the base of a cross-shaft in the churchyard. The hogback originally stood outside in a Christian churchyard, but the men and animals carved on its sides, in the tenth century, depict scenes from pagan Norse sagas. The cross-shaft by the entrance to the churchyard may be even older but is more evidently Christian: on one side is a seated figure with a halo, on the other what may be a house with a standing figure, apparently wrapped in a shroud. It probably represents the Raising of Lazarus or the Resurrection of Christ.

Hornby: St Margaret.

The church was begun in 1514, as the prominent Latin inscription over the west window states, by Sir Edward Stanley, the first Lord Mounteagle. He had led the Lancashire contingent at the battle of Flodden Field, and for his part in the English victory he was rewarded by Henry VIII with a title and some estates. The tower is remarkable for being octagonal and for the way in which the upper parts are twisted relative to the lower ones.

Lord Mounteagle also had the chancel built, and it too is unusual. It complements the tower by being semi-octagonal in plan, with the result that its large east window is placed between two smaller ones set at an angle — a feature which is as graceful inside as out. The interior of the nave was rebuilt in 1889, with arcades and a clerestory placed between early nineteenth-century walls, in a design of great distinction and discretion by Paley and Austin.

Kirkham: St Michael.

The best features of the church are the tower and spire which were added at the west end in 1844 to the designs of Edmund Sharpe. It is one of the finest steeples in the county, with deeply moulded buttresses at the corners of the tower, decorative details which become progressively richer as the tower's height increases, and a recessed octagonal spire supported by small flying buttresses.

The interior too is worth a visit. The nave, which was rebuilt on its old foundations in 1822, has an impressively wide unaisled space under a panelled ceiling which appears to be supported by a series of shallow wooden arches. There are also some features from the old church, like the brass chandelier (whose splendid curly supports are, however, modern) and a few monuments to the Cliftons of Lytham Hall.

Lancaster: Priory Church of St Mary.

The finest medieval church in the county is St Mary's in Lancaster, now known as the Priory Church because it stands on the site of Lancashire's first monastery. This was a priory of Benedictine monks, established by Roger of Poitou in 1094 and subordinated to the abbot of St Martin's Abbey at Sées in Normandy.

Most of the present church was built in the fifteenth century, after Henry V had disbanded the original monastic community — as an 'alien priory' — in 1413 during the Hundred Years War with France. The estates whose produce and rents had supported the priory were confiscated from the abbey of Sées and given to Syon Abbey, which the king had recently founded near London. In return, a new parish church was built at the abbey's expense. Its size must reflect the extent of the medieval parish of Lancaster, but the scale of the building is probably due to the self-esteem of Syon Abbey.

The church is faced almost all over with well dressed stone and gives the impression of being built to a single design; it is only inside that one notices that the pillars and clerestory windows beyond the chancel arch are more richly fashioned than those in the nave. Three fine Georgian chandeliers hang from gilded supports and there are several interesting eighteenth-century monuments in the aisles. To the north of the north aisle stands the chapel built in 1903 to commemorate the

St Margaret's church, Hornby.

officers and men of the King's Own Royal Regiment who had died in the Boer War. Hanging from its walls is one of the largest collections of regimental colours in Britain.

The church's greatest treasure is its set of fourteen wooden choir stalls which were carved about 1345. Each stall has a magnificent canopy, sumptuously carved with leaves set around and above flamboyant traceried panels, each different from its neighbour and separated from it by a richly crocketed pinnacle. There are at least a hundred little heads and faces carved among the panels. Ten of the stalls have their misericords, and all of them are decorated with attractive tapestry backs and cushions, whose motifs emphasise the links between the church and the community.

The tall tower, which forms the climax of the view of the castle and the church on their hill, was a replacement of the medieval tower and was constructed between 1753 and 1755. It is the oldest example in Lancashire of the Gothic Revival, that is the revival of decorative motifs from the middle ages.

Left: *The Georgian Gothic tower of Lancaster Priory.*

Below: *St Michael's church, Much Hoole.*

Lancaster: Roman Catholic Cathedral of St Peter.

St Peter's was built in 1859, to the design of Edward Paley, as a parish church but it has all the grandeur which one associates with a bishop's church. It became the cathedral in 1924, and its tower and spire are perhaps the finest in the county.

Inside the church, the chancel is vaulted (in wood) and still retains much of its original painted decoration and all of its fine stained glass representing Christ in Majesty; the west window, which shows the Last Judgement, is equally good. The finest decorative feature is the triptych, tucked away in the south transept, which used to stand behind the high altar. It was designed in 1909 by Giles Gilbert Scott, the architect of Liverpool's Anglican cathedral, and is beautifully carved and painted with scenes relating to the Crucifixion.

Much Hoole: St Michael.

The church is dated 1628 on the doorway inside its porch, and for nearly a century it was a simple brick building on a stone plinth. The interior, too, is simple, with box-pews, an early nineteenth-century gallery and a tall-backed pulpit with a sounding board, dated 1695. All this simplicity was made more sophisticated in 1722, when the slender tower was built to the west of the church, with its east wall resting within the church on an arch carried by two sturdy Tuscan columns. These are repeated as the main motif on the west front.

On the north face of the tower is a clock which serves as a memorial to Jeremiah Horrocks. He was the curate here when, on 24th November 1639, he became the first person ever to witness what astronomers call the Transit of Venus — the passing of the planet in front of the face of the sun. This was a significant event in man's evolving appreciation of his place in the universe, for it helped to prove the theory that the planets revolve around the sun, and not around the earth. The house where Horrocks saw this — Carr House, Bretherton — is dated 1613 and stands a little to the south, by the junction of the A59 and the B5247.

Newchurch-in-Pendle: St Mary.

Rebuilt in 1740, St Mary's church was probably 'new' in the early sixteenth century, when it was built for the people of the surrounding hamlets, which were developing from cattle farms established earlier on the edge of Pendle Forest. The plain unbuttressed tower, dated both 1653 and 1712, has an oval feature on the west face which is locally nicknamed the Eye of God. The interior is more pleasing with its fine chandelier, its Venetian east window and its six-bay arcade of

The towers of Ormskirk church.

Doric columns; this is unusual, too, because of the quality of its stonework, which is not dressed smooth but is slightly fluted on each face, so that there is a delicate play of light and shade across the surfaces of the columns and arches.

Ormskirk: St Peter and St Paul.

This stately church has both a spire, which is like the one at Halsall (see above), and a tower — a strange partnership. Local stories tell that they were built by two quarrelsome sisters, but the spire is about a hundred years older than the tower, which was built to house the bells of Burscough Priory after the Dissolution.

Inside, the church is largely a Victorian rebuilding, but there is a twelfth-century window in the chancel, and the Derby Chapel in the south-east corner contains four fifteenth-century effigies which are said to be those of the first Earl of Derby, his two wives and the third Earl; like the bells, they must have come from Burscough Priory.

Pilling: Old St John.

Old St John's church, which stands in what is still the parish graveyard, is no longer used for regular worship, since it was replaced in 1887 by Paley and Austin's fine church of St

Old St John's church, Pilling.

John about 200 yards to the north. It is now in the care of the Redundant Churches Fund, because it is virtually unchanged since its completion in 1717 and was not spoilt in Victorian times by 'restoration'.

It was built of the local soft red sandstone, with dressings of the harder gritstone. Inside, everything appears to be original, except for the north and west galleries on their timber columns, which probably date from the early nineteenth century. The floor is flagged, the walls are limewashed, the pews are of unvarnished oak and provide no more than a seat, a back and a pair of ends; there are a couple of box-pews for the 'better' families; the pulpit is a three-decker with simple panels, and there is a railing of turned balusters to protect the communion table. It is a time capsule of a simpler, less pretentious, though probably more bigoted age.

Pleasington: St Mary and St John the Baptist (Roman Catholic).

This church was built in 1819 as a thank-offering by the local squire, John Butler; this perhaps explains the boldness of the architecture some ten years before the Catholic Emancipation Act, but Lancashire has always been a strongly Catholic county. The church was designed by John Palmer, who knew a great deal about medieval architecture. His intention was to introduce into the church 'the different styles of architecture that prevailed in the kingdom from the days of King Ethelbert down to Henry VIII': the west doorway is modelled on the entrance to the chapter house at Whalley Abbey, and the rose window above would grace any French cathedral. Inside, there are tall arcades and clerestory windows, and the whole building has a lath and plaster vault with medallions showing scenes from the life of Christ above the central aisle.

Poulton-le-Fylde: St Chad.

The chancel of this church was built in 1868 with an apse, to look as though it had been built in the twelfth century; its tower was built in the early seventeenth century but could have been built at any time in the previous 150 years. Only the nave, which was completed in 1753 at the expense of Roger and Margaret Hesketh, was reasonably in fashion when it was built. Its classical facade on the side facing the Market Square is virtually symmetrical, with two tall central windows flanked by Doric doorways, with oval windows over them and another window to the side.

Inside, the nave has a single overall roof and no subdivisions except for the widely spaced Doric columns carrying the gallery which runs around three sides. This has a panelled front with the original candle holders and is approached up a fine staircase in the north-west corner.

Rawtenstall: Goodshaw Old Baptist Chapel. English Heritage. 2 miles north of Rawtenstall on minor road off A56.

This former chapel was built in 1760 and then extended forward in the early nineteenth century. There are galleries on three sides, supported on cast iron columns and dating from this period, as do the box-pews and the raised pulpit, which is between the two doors and above the singers' pew. The address of the keyholder is displayed at the chapel.

Ribchester: St Wilfrid.

The church stands within the earthworks of the Roman fort on its riverside site (see chapter 3). The nave and chancel were built in the thirteenth century, and the chancel still has its original lancet windows in the east end and south side, although the latter is disfigured by an inserted Victorian window. The tower, like so many in Lancashire, dates from the late fifteenth century.

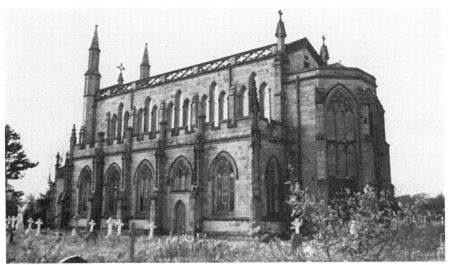

Pleasington Catholic church.

On the north side of the interior is an interesting chantry chapel, the Dutton Quire, which dates from the first half of the fourteenth century. This has a series of windows (with a few fragments of old glass) which provide a textbook of tracery design of that period. The roof of the Dutton Quire is almost certainly original, since it has no beam at the ridge but is stiffened along its length by a lower beam carried on brackets at either end and on a crown post in the centre. All the other roofs date from around 1500 and are more normal in their construction. Other pieces of woodwork which are of interest are the seventeenth-century pulpit, the eighteenth-century box-pews and the west gallery, which is dated 1736 and supported on stone columns which are said to be Roman.

Goodshaw Old Baptist Chapel, Rawtenstall.

23

Slaidburn: St Andrew.

This late medieval church is of no great beauty but its fittings are of considerable interest, having remained virtually unchanged since the eighteenth century. Most of the nave is filled with seventeenth-century pews; there are also Georgian box-pews and a fine three-decker pulpit, installed in 1740. Most such pulpits were reduced in height in Victorian times, when box-pews were removed to restore a more medieval appearance to churches, so this one is something of a rarity; the only other one in the county is at Pilling (see above). The parish clerk led the congregation's responses from the bottom stall, while the parson conducted the service from the middle tier, or lectern, and when it was time for him to preach he climbed the well balustraded stair to the pulpit, which stands on four columns and has a sounding board to enable his voice to be heard more clearly.

To the east of the pulpit is the most interesting feature of the church: the Jacobean chancel screen, which is unique in the county.

St Wilfrid's church, Ribchester.

It was placed there in the 1630s, in response to Archbishop Laud's orders that the Church of England should revert to something approaching the style of worship of pre-Reformation days, with a screen to separate the priest in his chancel from the people in their nave. This screen is a fine piece with tapering square uprights, closely carved with geometric patterns and carrying semicircular arches which support an openwork balustrade.

Tunstall: St John.

The church now stands alone, in a graveyard full of yew trees, but it probably marks the site of the original village. The nave, chancel, sturdy tower and two-storey porch were built in about 1415 at the expense of Sir Thomas Tunstall of Thurland Castle, whose effigy lies in the south-east chapel. The glass in the east windows came from the Low Countries and was made in the fifteenth or sixteenth century; the centrepiece shows Christ giving the keys of Heaven to St Peter and is flanked by older panels with the Madonna and Child and St Anthony.

Tunstall church was the model for Brocklebridge church in Charlotte Brontë's novel *Jane Eyre*. She and her sisters were unhappy pupils at the Clergy Daughters' School, founded in 1823 by the vicar of Tunstall. Every Sunday they had to walk from Cowan Bridge (where the school building still stands by the A65 just north of the bridge) and eat their packed lunch, between the services, in the room above the porch.

Upholland: St Thomas the Martyr.

This, the only monastic church still standing in Lancashire, was built around 1330 by the Bishop of Lichfield, in whose diocese Lancashire south of the Ribble was then included. The nave of the present church was the monks' choir, and the present chancel dates only from 1882. The tower was built in the fifteenth century, and on a smaller scale than was originally intended. It is therefore something of an anticlimax, but the present nave, even though it has no clerestory windows, is a spacious and stately building with boldly modelled pillars and arches and tall windows in the aisles.

Whalley: St Mary.

St Mary's is the finest thirteenth-century church in the county, and one of the most interesting of any date. It stands close to the ruins of the abbey (see chapter 3) but is at least a hundred years older, while the ancient sanctity of the site is proven by the presence in the churchyard of three pre-Conquest crosses.

The nave of the present church was probably built around a smaller, older one, the north aisle being built before the south,

The Friends' Meeting House at Yealand Conyers.

because its piers are round, whereas the southern ones are octagonal. Although the five-light east window dates from the fifteenth century and its glass, depicting the arms of local families, dates from 1816, the chancel is also a fine example of thirteenth-century work, with shallow gabled buttresses and narrow lancet windows. The tower, the windows in the aisles and the clerestory windows in the nave were all built in the fifteenth century, as were the roofs, the one in the nave being particularly fine.

The woodwork is the best feature of the interior, not merely in the roofs, and the seventeenth-century pews but also in the screens, especially those around the pews of the rival families, the Nowells of Read Hall and the Starkies of Huntroyde, which stand to the south and north respectively. The finest woodwork of all is in the spikily canopied choir stalls from the abbey, datable by the initials W.W. to the years 1418-34. These were altered in 1866 but are substantially authentic with their detached shafts and vaulted canopies; they also have the finest set of misericords in the county. The undersides of the seats are carved with all manner of motifs, of which only some are religious. Several — like St George killing the dragon, a fox running away with a goose, and a woman hitting a man with a frying pan — are carved in a very spirited fashion. At the west end is a gallery, built in 1813 to carry the fine organ, which was made originally for St Mary's church, Lancaster, in 1728.

Yealand Conyers: Friends' Meeting House.

Friends' meeting houses date back further than any other nonconformist places of worship in Lancashire and the meeting house at Yealand Conyers, which is set in a well tended graveyard with regular rows of simple headstones and the feel of a cottage garden, was originally built in 1692. It was damaged by fire in the mid eighteenth century and partly rebuilt; only the datestone on the porch and an upper window to the right reveal its pre-Georgian origins. The two doors are well panelled — though badly disfigured with well carved initials, including one dated 1775 — and lead to the meeting room itself, which has twelve-pane sash windows, as in a house, and well made panelling with fluted pilasters.

25

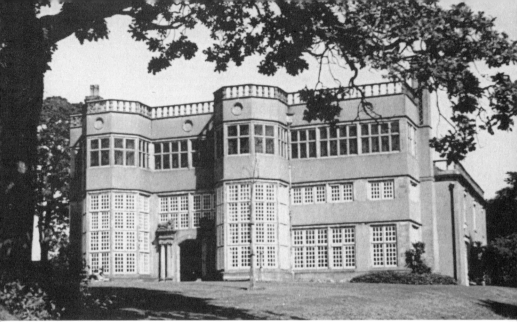

Astley Hall — 'more glass than wall'.

5
Historic houses and gardens

Lancashire is not well known for its country houses and is unfortunate since Lytham Hall and Scarisbrick Hall, its two finest houses — in purely architectural terms, at least — are not normally open to the public. Despite this, the county has much to offer to anyone who appreciates stately homes, and those houses which are open to visitors are described here. Intending visitors are advised to find out the opening times before travelling.

Astley Hall, Chorley. Telephone: 02572 62166. 1 mile north-west of Chorley town centre, off A6.

The rhyming description of Hardwick Hall — 'more glass than wall' — applies equally well to the south (or entrance) wing of Astley Hall and its virtually unbroken screen of windows, which was originally built in the 1620s of brick with stone dressings.

The most interesting rooms in the south wing are the two-storey hall, which one sees on entering, and the long gallery which is above it. The ceiling of the hall is its most remarkable feature but dates from the 1660s rather than the 1620s. It was made to celebrate the marriage of Margaret Charnock to Sir Peter Brooke in 1666, because the coats of arms of both families are in the frieze along with cupids in the compartments between the beams. The ceiling of the drawing room (to the

right of the hall) is even more boldly moulded: it has a great oval wreath with twisted scrolls and flowers, within which are four shells and two cherubs holding garlands.

Back in the hall, the fascinating series of painted panels representing all manner of 'heroes' must date from the 1620s. These heroes are not merely Protestants like Queen Elizabeth and Sir Francis Drake but include Philip II of Spain, who launched the Armada, and Islamic soldiers like Tamerlane and Mohammed II, who captured Constantinople. The unknown Jacobean gentleman who commissioned these portraits must have been a soldier who admired them all as fellow leaders of men.

The staircase, which has a fine balustrade carved with cherubs and rich scrolls of acanthus, leads eventually to the long gallery. This is the most remarkable of the early seventeenth-century rooms in the house and runs the full length of the top floor, with an unbroken expanse of windows on the west, south and east sides. Almost equally remarkable is the shuffleboard table, standing on twenty turned legs; it is nearly 24 feet (7 metres) long and must have been built in the room.

Astley Hall is also Chorley's museum and has, as well as many items of local interest, a large quantity of good seventeenth-century furniture, especially a very fine four-poster bed, supposedly used by Cromwell in 1648.

Browsholme Hall, near Clitheroe. Telephone: 025486 330. 4 miles north-west of Clitheroe, off B6243.

Browsholme Hall could hardly be called a great country house; an important part of its attraction is that it is still a family home and visitors are normally shown around by a member of the Parker family, who have lived there for six hundred years and took their surname from their office as hereditary keepers of the deer park in the royal hunting Forest of Bowland.

The house was built in 1507 and was re-fronted after 1603, with a fine display of the three orders of classical columns around the doorway, when Thomas Parker bought the freehold of the estate from the Crown. The left wing was partly rebuilt in 1807 to the designs of Jeffrey Wyatt for Thomas Lister Parker. He, like his friend Charles Towneley of Towneley Hall (see below), was a notable antiquary and one of the first people to take an interest in Elizabethan furniture. The hall into which one enters is virtually as he left it, with old tables, chairs, dressers, weapons and armour.

Several of the other rooms contain further pieces of old oak furniture and panelling — some original, some Victorian copies — but the most attractive rooms are Wyatt's dining and drawing rooms, which retain their Regency elegance and contain some fine eighteenth-century furniture and an extensive collection of pleasing family portraits.

Gawthorpe Hall, Padiham. Telephone: 0282 78511. National Trust. 1 mile east of Padiham, off A671.

Gawthorpe Hall is the best example in Lancashire of an Elizabethan country house 'restored' in a flush of Victorian enthusiasm for the good old days of merry England, and the National Trust has boldly refurbished it to stress its Victorian, rather than its Elizabethan, character. It was built between 1600 and 1605 for Lawrence Shuttleworth and it is likely that Robert Smythson, who had designed Hardwick Hall, also had a hand in the design of Gawthorpe.

Despite the Victorian changes, it is still possible, in three or four of the rooms, to get a good idea of what Gawthorpe was like when originally built. The least-changed room lies to the left of the entrance hall; though now called the Drawing Room and refurnished in the mid Victorian manner, it was originally the family dining room. The panelling is typical of the early seventeenth century, with square panels enriched with high-quality marquetry of stylised foliage; above the panels is a delightful plaster frieze with a variety of little birds and animals, heraldic beasts, mermaids and men and women in contemporary costume. Overall

Gawthorpe Hall: the Drawing-Room ceiling.

is a fine plaster ceiling with flat ribs, pendants and panels containing vine trails and bunches of grapes.

The long gallery on the top floor is also relatively unchanged. It has a similar but less ornate ceiling and a chimneypiece with the arms of James I and inscriptions in Latin and English to remind the Shuttleworths to honour the king, fear God, do good and seek peace. There is now also a fine collection of portraits, from the National Portrait Gallery, of prominent people connected with politics and the arts in the later Stuart court.

The Shuttleworths left Gawthorpe around 1670, and it was hardly lived in again by the family until around 1850 when Sir James and Lady Janet Kay-Shuttleworth called upon the architect Sir Charles Barry, then working on the new Houses of Parliament, to refurbish their house. What is now called the Dining Room, though it was originally the hall, is largely a Victorian room, with a splendid chimneypiece carved with the various coats of arms of the Shuttleworth family during the centuries. The fine wooden staircase, reached through a solidly built stone screen, was also designed by Barry. It leads to the top floor and then to the tower, which was raised by Barry to emphasise his mistaken belief that the house had originally been a pele tower.

Gawthorpe Hall is a house of major art-historical significance, but it also has a remarkable collection of needlework, ranging from lace to tapestry, altar frontals to articles of clothing, which was made by the last occupant of the hall, Miss Rachel Kay-Shuttleworth. She had a lifelong interest both in textiles and in the crafts used to make them, and she was also a very talented needlewoman, as can be seen in the beautiful hangings and counterpane which she embroidered during the First World War for a bed now in the Huntroyde Room.

Hoghton Tower, Hoghton, near Preston PR5 0SH. Telephone: 025485 2986. 6 miles south-east of Preston, off A675.

Standing on top of a 300 foot (90 metre) escarpment and looking rather like a small castle, Hoghton Tower is really little more than a manor house built around a pair of courtyards and approached through a fortified gatehouse. It was begun in the early 1560s by Sir Thomas Hoghton and, perhaps, not finished until the early seventeenth century by his nephew Sir Richard, who was one of the first baronets to be created in 1611.

In August 1617 Sir Richard was the host to James I when he paid a memorable visit to Hoghton. After dinner in the Banqueting Hall, which stands on the left in the inner courtyard, the King dubbed a loin of beef 'Sir Loin', to the amusement of his assembled courtiers.

The tower between the courtyards — which gave the house its name — was blown up during a short siege in 1642 and later demolished. The Hoghton family moved out in the eighteenth century and the house was thereby spared from any Georgian remodelling, but it had to be substantially restored in the later nineteenth century, when the family returned — now calling themselves de Hoghton. The restoration work was very carefully done, largely by Paley and Austin. There is a fine staircase of the late seventeenth century and, in the ballroom, attractive nineteenth-century panelling by Gillow. There is pleasing furniture and a fine collection of dolls' houses, while from the gardens behind the house there are splendid views. Visitors can also see the underground passages and large wine cellar, and the Tudor well house with its machinery in working order.

Leighton Hall, Yealand Conyers, near Carnforth. Telephone: 052473 4474. 3 miles north of Carnforth, off A6.

Leighton Hall is the most beautiful country house of the early Gothic Revival in Lancashire. The house is built of a very white limestone and sits in a half-saucer of tree-framed pasture land, backed by the Furness Fells; on a fine day the view, as one turns into the drive, is sheer delight. There are other attractions as well, since on every fine day the hawks and falcons from the Leighton collection put on a remarkable flying display.

The owners of Leighton have always been Roman Catholics and during the 1745 rebellion the house was damaged by government troops, so George Towneley, a relative of the Towneleys of Towneley Hall (see below), decided to rebuild it. The pretty Gothic disguise was applied to the Georgian house probably after 1822 when the house and estate were purchased by Richard Gillow. He was the son of the furniture designer of the same name and had sold the family business and retired to live the life of a country gentleman. The house is still lived in by his descendants. The final stage in the gothicisation of Leighton Hall came in 1870, when Paley and Austin added the tower and the cross-wing on the left, to create a most picturesque design of controlled asymmetry.

Several of the main rooms are decorated in a Gothic manner, and the entrance hall is perhaps the most beautiful room in the house. It has a screen of three shallow cast iron arches on cast iron clustered columns which separate the hall from the gracefully sweeping stone staircase. This has balusters which are miniature versions of the columns of the screen. To the right of the hall is the dining room, a darkly panelled room with windows like those

Rufford Old Hall.

in the Shire Hall in Lancaster (see chapter 3). The most attractive feature is the seven panels painted with Romantic landscapes, but, as in every room in the house, there are good pieces of Gillow furniture.

Rivington Terraced Gardens, Rivington, near Chorley. Telephone: Great House Barn Information Centre, 0204 691549. East of Rivington Hall, 4 miles south-east of Chorley.

In the early twentieth century Lord Leverhulme built Roynton Cottage here and created a large private garden now called Rivington Terraced Gardens. It was laid out to the designs of the great landscape architect Thomas Mawson, who was keen to accept the challenge of creating a garden on the wild and windswept moorland.

The cottage burnt down in 1913 and its successor was demolished in 1948 but the gardens survive and, after passing into the care of the North West Water Authority, have been restored to something approaching their original condition. Since they face west over the reservoirs, they are now very attractive for an afternoon visit and are dotted with features like staircases, miniature waterfalls, garden shelters, a seven-arched bridge built of small stones and what is called the Pigeon Tower, a tall, thin summerhouse built in 1910, a landmark for miles around.

Rufford Old Hall, Rufford. Telephone: 0704 821254. National Trust. 6 miles north-northeast of Ormskirk, on A59.

This pretty building, which marries timber and brickwork in a most picturesque fashion, contains the finest medieval timber-framed hall in the county and one of the best in England. It was built towards the end of the fifteenth century by a member of the Hesketh family, which owned the house until 1936. The medieval house now exists in a much truncated form, since the family wing (to the right of the bay window) has disappeared and the service wing (behind the gable to the left) was in part rebuilt in the early nineteenth century, though it does contain a medieval roof. A visit begins in the brick-built wing, dated 1662, but the glory of the house is the great open hall.

This is entered under what is called a spere truss, in which two enormous carved wooden pillars are set about 4 feet (1.2 metres) inside the main walls to support a screen and thus reduce the draughts from the now unused doorways, which face each other. Between the pillars stands a richly panelled, theoretically movable screen with three outlandish twisted pinnacles, added later.

The hall is decorated with an exuberance which grows with the height from the floor. The walls themselves are fairly plain, but the four hammer-beam trusses have angels car-

Samlesbury Hall.

rying shields and support arches with big bosses, carved with coats of arms. Within the roof itself are three tiers of windbraces which form quatrefoils. At the further (or upper) end, where the table for the lord, his family and guests once stood, the ceiling is coved to form a sort of canopy (above which a priest-hole was found); on the right is a tall bay window, added after the hall was built, as a further status symbol.

The rest of the house contains attractive displays of costumes and also an interesting local folk museum. There is a large garden alongside the canal and a picnic area.

Samlesbury Hall, Samlesbury, near Preston. Telephone: 025481 2010. 4 miles east of Preston on A677.

Samlesbury Hall is the most striking 'black and white' house in Lancashire, but the most photogenic part — the south wing, through which one enters the house — is not the oldest and was not built until the 1540s. Perhaps a century older than this is the hall, which stands to the right of the bay window; it is somewhat shorter than when it was originally built. Two of its five trusses are cruck trusses — undeniably impressive, as they rise up from the ground in a pointed sweep to the ridge, so that they (and not the walls) carry the weight of the roof. The fireplace appears to date from the early sixteenth century, as do the bay window and the screen, which was moved during a Victorian restoration to stand next to the window. The screen, as it now stands, is a hotchpotch of medieval and Jacobean wood-

work, with an inscription dated 1523 and three grotesque pinnacles like those at Rufford Old Hall.

The south wing was built by Sir Thomas Southworth to contain a private parlour, with a fireplace dated 1545 and a richly beamed ceiling. Beyond this is the chapel, and above these rooms is a fine long room, originally subdivided, which would have provided bedrooms. All of these rooms had the by then fashionable fireplace in the wall, and, outside, one of the chimneys carries the coat of arms of Sir Thomas, so that everyone should know who had built these striking status symbols. He built the wall between the stacks in brick, because, after the dissolution of Whalley Abbey, he was able to buy a number of fine stone windows, which could not be easily fitted into a timber-framed wall.

Stonyhurst College, Stonyhurst BB6 9PZ. 3 miles north-west of Whalley, off B6243.

Stonyhurst is not normally open to the public, since it has been a Roman Catholic boarding school since 1794 but, fortunately, a minor road from Hurst Green forms the first part of the great entrance drive and brings one quite close to the front of the house. This was designed in 1592, rather as Hoghton Tower (see above) had been a generation earlier, around a courtyard with the hall on the further side. None of this can be seen from the road, but the great gatehouse is unmistakable. It is basically late medieval in concept but is faced with four tiers of classical columns, arranged one above the other just as the Romans had done. Another Roman motif — the triumphal arch, which can be seen within the lowest storey — was an assertion of the power and pride of Sir Richard Shireburne, who set about rebuilding the home of his ancestors in 1592.

A century later Sir Nicholas Shireburne, the last of his line to be lord of the manor, had some work carried out which can be seen from the road: the two octagonal turrets topped with domes and eagles, which crown the gatehouse, and the pair of 'canals' which flank the drive and are part of the formal gardens which were laid out by James II's gardener, Henry Wise. He also built the fine Shireburne Almshouses at Hurst Green.

The Elizabethan core of the college buildings is now flanked on either side by harmonious additions of the nineteenth and twentieth centuries, notably the church of St Peter (1835). The splendid south front was among the extensions made in the late nineteenth century.

Towneley Hall, Burnley BB11 3RQ. Telephone: 0282 24213. 1 mile south-east of Burnley town centre, off A646.

From the outside Towneley Hall is fairly dour, with a vaguely medieval appearance, representing — basically — the medieval hall and two extended cross-wings. Passing through the porch with its worn wooden door dated 1530, one suddenly finds oneself, however, in the middle of the long side of a two-storey hall, lined out with tall fluted Ionic

pilasters carrying a cornice, above which the ceiling is richly decorated with elaborate plasterwork. This is the finest early eighteenth-century room in Lancashire, built for Richard Towneley soon after 1725 and decorated by the Italian plasterers Francesco Vassali and Martino Quadri, who were working in several houses in the north of England at that time. They were doubtless chosen because they could turn a big space into an impressive space, suggestive of the power and cultural discernment of their patron. To the left, the fireplace has a richly scrolled overmantel which serves as a pedestal for a copy of the statue of the Medici Venus, while the opposite fireplace carries the Dancing Faun; these were two favourite statues among Georgian gentry. In the coves between the attic windows there are playing cherubs; medallions of Roman emperors hang between the pilasters and Richard Towneley's coat of arms, with eighteen quarterings, hangs proudly over the doorway.

Vassali and Quadri also did the plasterwork for a new staircase on the left of the hall, which leads to the Tudor long gallery. This stair climbs up around an open well and has an excellent wrought iron balustrade, which is thought to be by Robert Bakewell, one of the most famous smiths of the eighteenth century.

The Towneleys were a Catholic family, and their chapel contains a splendid early sixteenth-century Flemish altarpiece with scenes of Christ's crucifixion carved in wood under

Stonyhurst College.

31

traceried canopies of great delicacy. It was brought to the house by Charles Towneley, one of the most learned collectors in the eighteenth century. In the art gallery on the second floor there is a portrait of him, with his dog and friends, among his famous collection of antique sculptures, which were bought after his death in 1805 by the British Museum, where they can still be seen.

Charles Towneley had a suite of rooms laid out in the left-hand wing, but they were destroyed in the early nineteenth century and replaced by two Regency rooms, designed by Jeffrey Wyatt in 1812: the first one is used for exhibitions, while the second is more richly decorated, and furnished as it might have been at that period.

Towneley Hall is Burnley's museum and has some interesting exhibits to appeal to most tastes: local crafts and industries in the former brewhouse, attractive watercolours including some by Turner, prehistoric flints, and seventeenth-century furniture; but nothing is more beautiful than the priests' vestments from Whalley Abbey (see chapter 3).

Turton Tower, Chapeltown Road, Turton, near Bolton BL7 0HG. Telephone: 0204 852203. Just south of Capeltown, off B6391.

Turton Tower was originally a low three-storey stone pele tower, perhaps built by William Orrell who inherited the Turton estate in 1420. Sometime in the sixteenth century two cruck-framed buildings were added to provide kitchens and service rooms. These survive in part, to the right of the present entrance, though from the outside they are disguised by later stone cladding.

In 1596 another William Orrell raised the height of the tower, creating the spacious rooms which one sees today. He probably also added the timber-framed two-storey entrance porch and replaced a stone spiral stair with an open-well staircase of timber. His building schemes ruined the family fortunes and in 1628 his son was forced to sell the estate to Humphrey Chetham, the famous Manchester merchant. Chetham's heirs and, later, several generations of tenant farmers lived in the house until it was sold in 1835 to James Kay, a prosperous local cotton spinner who had long cherished the ambition of being lord of the manor of Turton and restoring the Tower to its former glory.

Kay was responsible for widening the staircase block and for transforming the service wing with stone Dutch gables. Much of the interior in its present form is also Kay's work, but he did use old materials like the original staircase balustrade, the seventeenth-century panelling in the Drawing Room and the early eighteenth-century panelling in the Dining Room, which was salvaged from the nearby Middleton Hall. The Tower contains a museum, which includes some attractive pieces of seventeenth-century furniture, armour and weapons.

Towneley Hall, Burnley.

Pendle Heritage Centre, Barrowford.

6
Museums and art galleries

ACCRINGTON

Haworth Art Gallery, Haworth Park, Manchester Road, Accrington BB5 2JS. Telephone: 0254 33782.

Established in an attractive Jacobean-style house built in 1909, the gallery is the permanent home of an internationally famous collection of 130 pieces of beautiful glassware, ranging from lamps to vases, paperweights to mosaics and tiles, made around 1900 in the Tiffany Studios in New York. To complement them a collection of contemporary glass has been started. There are also some good early English watercolours. Admission is free.

BARNOLDSWICK

Bancroft Mill Engine Museum, Gillans Lane, off Colne Road, Barnoldswick. Telephone: 0282 814586.

Bancroft Mill was the last weaving shed to be built in the present county, in 1922. When it was closed in 1978, the fine 600 horsepower cross-compound steam engine was preserved and is regularly run. An associated exhibition displays tools and documents relating to the weaving industry.

BARROWFORD

Pendle Heritage Centre, Park Hill, Barrowford, Nelson BB9 6JQ. Telephone: 0282 695366.

Both a local museum and a local studies centre, the Pendle Heritage Centre is accommodated in a seventeenth-century farmhouse which was built and extended by the Bannister family, from whom Roger Bannister, the first man to run a mile in under four minutes, is descended. The history of the family, the house and the Pendle area — its farming, its transport facilities and its witches — is interestingly portrayed. Two rooms are furnished as farmhouse parlours of the seventeenth and nineteenth centuries; there is an eighteenth-century walled garden and, in the barn, a small agricultural museum. Over the road, the Tollhouse (see chapter 7) is also part of the centre.

BLACKBURN

Blackburn Museum and Art Gallery, Museum Street, Blackburn BB1 7AJ. Telephone: 0254 667130.

A fascinating series of bas-reliefs around the corner from the main door shows mid Victorian mill girls and metalworkers, merchants in the Levant, a man honing a scythe and a shepherd in a smock. Inside the museum there are displays on the East Lancashire Regiment and on local history and natural history; but the finest exhibits are based on gifts from local industrialists: Japanese prints, Eastern Orthodox icons and the Hart Collection of beautiful medieval illuminated manuscripts and early printed books. Admission is free.

Lewis Museum of Textile Machinery, Exchange Street, Blackburn. Telephone: 0254 667130.

This is the most accessible display in the county of early textile machinery, ranging from the traditional spinning wheel and handloom to the nineteenth-century Lancashire loom, by way of Kay's fly shuttle, Hargreaves's spinning jenny, Arkwright's waterframe and Crompton's mule. Admission is free.

BURNLEY

Towneley Hall Art Gallery and Museums, Towneley Park, Burnley BB11 3RQ. Telephone: 0282 24213.

Towneley Hall is both a stately home and the borough's museum (see chapter 5). Admission is free.

Weavers' Triangle Visitor Centre, 85a Manchester Road, Burnley BB11 1JZ. Telephone: 0282 30055.

The tollhouse built at the Manchester Road wharf of the Leeds and Liverpool Canal (see chapter 7) is the home of a small but interesting display, which interprets the influence of the canal on the development of Burnley and of its cotton industry.

CARNFORTH

Steamtown, off Warton Road, Carnforth. Telephone: 0524 732100.

Steamtown, established in what used to be British Rail's last operational steam locomotive depot, is one of Lancashire's three working museums, complete with its offices and workshops, which are still in use for the maintenance and restoration of steam locomotives. It also has a vacuum-operated turntable and a coaling tower which is now unique in Britain. It is most famous as the home of more than thirty locomotives, including two from the continent and ranging from humble tank engines to famous express locomotives such as *Lord Nelson, Sir Nigel Gresley* and *Flying Scotsman*, which are regularly in steam and pulling trains. There is also a 15 inch (38 cm) gauge railway with scaled-down engines and coaches which run on a mile-long track, plus a model railway layout in a bus! A single admission charge, which varies according to the services on offer, allows unlimited rides on the trains.

CHORLEY

Astley Hall Museum and Art Gallery, Astley Park, Chorley. Telephone: 02572 62166.

Astley Hall was built as a country house (see chapter 5) and is now the borough's museum.

CLITHEROE

Clitheroe Castle Museum, Castle Hill, Clitheroe BB7 1BA. Telephone: 0200 24635.

Standing within the once fortified enclosure of Clitheroe Castle (see chapter 3), the eighteenth-century steward's house now accommodates an interesting museum of local history, with the reconstructed workshops of a clogmaker and a printer and a well presented display on the geology and fossils of the area.

FLEETWOOD

Fleetwood Museum, Dock Street, Fleetwood FY7 6AQ. Telephone: 03917 6621.

The museum is in two interrelated sections: one on the history of Fleetwood, which began its life as the first seaside resort and port accessible by railway; and the second on the fishing industries, both inshore and deep-sea, which have been based in the town since the 1880s. There are displays of nets and other tackle used for fishing salmon and shrimps in Morecambe Bay, as well as models of ships and trawls and a full-scale mock-up of a trawler bridge.

FULWOOD

Museum of the Loyal Regiment, Fulwood Barracks, Watling Street Road, Fulwood, Preston PR2 4AA. Telephone: 0772 716543 extension 2362.

The museum of the Loyal Regiment (North Lancashire) contains uniforms, weapons and equipment, and also the regimental archives, from the eighteenth century to the present, in the setting of Fulwood Barracks, which were built in 1848. Admission is free, but a donation is sought.

GISBURN

Gisburn Steam Museum, Todber Caravan Park, Gisburn BB7 4JJ. Telephone: 02005 322.

This is a collection of rare steam road vehicles which have been renovated, including the only known example of a Howard traction engine, which dates from 1872. There is also a new fairground organ, which is believed to be the largest in the world. Admission is free but a donation to charity is sought.

HARLE SYKE

Queen Street Mill, Queen Street, Harle Syke, Burnley. Telephone: 0282 412555.

A visit to Queen Street Mill complements one to the museum at Helmshore (see below) because both are working museums. Queen Street Mill is now the only steam-powered weaving shed in Britain, where one can experience the sight, smell and deafening sounds of Lancashire looms at work and then contrast them with the tandem-compound steam engine, aptly named *Peace*, which provides the power with no more noise than the click of the valve-gear and the whirr of the flywheel. One can also buy 'union shirts' made from the cloth woven at the mill.

HELMSHORE
Museum of the Lancashire Textile Industry, Holcombe Road, Helmshore, Rossendale BB4 4NP. Telephone: 0706 226459.

At Helmshore, in contrast to Harle Syke (see above), one can follow the whole process of spinning, under the guidance of a former millworker, from the carding which straightens the fibres to the actual spinning on the eighty-year-old self-acting mules, which trundle back and forth across the floor and each time produce half a mile of yarn. The lower floor of what used to be Whitaker's Mill is occupied by displays which outline the rise and fall of the Lancashire textile industry and its associated industries.

One can also see an internationally important collection of early textile machines like an improved spinning jenny and the later version of Arkwright's water-frame from his mill at Cromford, Derbyshire.

The second mill at Helmshore, Higher Mill, is older; built in 1789, it may be the oldest mill in the county. It contains fulling stocks, where lengths of woollen cloth were soaked and pounded with heavy hammers to tighten the weave, and also a very fine mid nineteenth-century waterwheel, 18 feet (5.5 metres) in diameter, which can generate 50 horsepower.

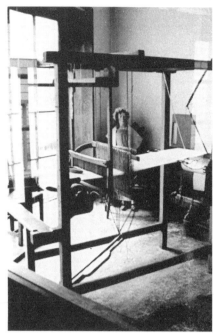

Above: *A traditional handloom at the Lewis Museum of Textile Machinery, Blackburn.*

Below: *Steamtown, Carnforth.*

35

The Old Custom House on St George's Quay, home of Lancaster Maritime Museum.

The Music Room, Lancaster.

LANCASTER

Ashton Memorial, Williamson Park, Wyresdale Road, Lancaster LA2 1UX. Telephone: 0524 33318.

Superbly restored and standing in a lovely park, this is now once more 'the grandest monument in England', its Portland stone and copper-covered dome resplendent on the hill. It was built to the designs of Sir John Belcher for Lord Ashton, the millionaire king of the linoleum industry, and opened to the public in October 1909 to commemorate his family and to remind the people of his native town of the benefits which two generations of Williamsons had bestowed on them. It now commemorates Lord Ashton's life and times in a free exhibition on the ground floor, and, in the upper room, the age in which he lived with a striking audio-visual presentation on the Edwardians. From the balconies there are splendid views over the Fylde and across Morecambe Bay to the Lakeland fells.

On the other side of the pebble-paved square from the memorial is the Butterfly House, which is the home of hundreds of exotic butterflies fluttering freely among tropical flowers and plants.

Cottage Museum, 15 Castle Hill, Lancaster. Telephone: 0524 64637.

In striking contrast to the fine Georgian town houses which surround it, this cottage — part of a house, dated 1739, which was divided into two dwellings around 1820 — has been furnished to give some idea of the relative discomfort in which a small craftsman and his family lived a few years before Queen Victoria came to the throne.

Judges' Lodging, Church Street, Lancaster LA1 1YS. Telephone: 0524 32808.

The Judges' Lodging is not merely a museum but also the oldest house in Lancaster. It was built in the 1620s for his own use by Thomas Covell, who was the Keeper of the castle for 48 years. The house was extended to the rear in 1675 by a later owner, Thomas Cole, whose badge of lions' heads can be seen at the front door. To the right of the entrance hall is the most attractive room in the house, which probably dates from the 1730s: it has oak panelling with fluted pilasters and a painted wall cupboard decorated with a shell motif.

Between 1826 and 1975 the house was used three times a year by the judges who came for the assizes — hence its name — and big extensions were built for them. Some of the rooms in the house are now laid out as they were when used by early Victorian judges and their staff, but most are dedicated to the two museums which the house now accommodates. These are the Gillow Museum, which contains displays on the history, tools and products of the celebrated Lancaster cabinet makers, and the Museum of Childhood, which displays the famous Barry Elder Collection of dolls, together with toys, games and a wide variety of exhibits relating to children, including a Victorian schoolroom.

Lancaster City Museum, Market Square, Lancaster LA1 1HT. Telephone: 0524 64637.

Established in the former town hall, which was completed in 1783, the City Museum's collections concentrate on the social and economic history of Lancaster and its area, with a fine collection of old photographs and three models of the town, based on its three oldest maps, which show it in 1610, 1778 and 1821. There are also some spectacular Roman finds, a seventh-century shroud and boat-shaped coffin which were found in 1973 near the Jubilee Tower and a special section with uniforms, medals and documents relating to the King's Own Royal (Lancaster) Regiment. Admission is free.

Lancaster Maritime Museum, Old Custom House, St George's Quay, Lancaster LA1 1RB. Telephone: 0524 64637.

This museum occupies the former custom house, which was designed by Richard Gillow and built in 1764, and part of the neighbouring warehouse on St George's Quay (see chapter 7). Its fascinating displays deal not merely with the history of the port of Lancaster and its links with the West Indies slave and sugar trade, but also with the Lancaster Canal and the *Waterwitch* packet, which sailed from Preston to Kendal in seven hours in the days before the railway. Other sections deal with more recent matters like the development of the port of Heysham and the exploitation of the Morecambe Bay gasfield.

Music Room, Sun Street, Lancaster. Telephone: 0524 60658.

The Music Room was built as a summerhouse in a garden belonging to what is now the Conservative Club in Church Street and presents in its first-floor room the most lavish display of early Georgian plasterwork in the

county. Above the fireplace stands the god Apollo with his lyre, flanked by two muses. On other walls are the other muses and musical instruments. In the ceiling is Ceres, the goddess of agriculture, surrounded by garlands of flowers and fruit and medallions bearing portraits of Roman emperors. The decoration is perhaps too crowded, but it shows off the plasterer's skill in an impressive manner. Admission is free.

LEYLAND
British Commercial Vehicle Museum, King Street, Leyland, Preston PR5 1LE. Telephone: 0772 451011.

Devoted to the history of British commercial vehicles, this is the largest museum of commercial vehicles in Europe, with over forty exhibits, including buses, trucks, vans, fire engines and the famous Popemobile. The museum traces the development of commercial road vehicles in Britain from the horse-drawn era through steam wagons and early petrol engines to the present day.

LYTHAM
Motive Power Museum, off Warton Road (A584), Lytham. Telephone: 0253 733122.

The collection contains not merely locomotives and railway rolling stock, but also road vehicles of different sorts. There is also a miniature railway.

PRESTON
Harris Museum and Art Gallery, Market Square, Preston PR1 2PP. Telephone: 0772 58248.

The Harris Museum and Art Gallery is a magnificent Greek Revival temple in the centre of Preston, towering above the bustle of the Market Square. A fine view of the interior can be seen from the rotunda on the ground floor. Rich collections of ceramics and glass and the very interesting gallery devoted to the history of Preston are on the first floor; above them is the art gallery, which includes seven small portraits by the eighteenth-century Preston painter, Arthur Devis. New costume and watercolour galleries open in 1989. Admission is free.

Lancashire County and Regimental Museum, Stanley Street, Preston PR1 4YP. Telephone: 0772 264075.

The old County Sessions House of 1825 is the home of this museum, which evokes the history not merely of several of the county's regiments — The Queen's Lancashire Regiment (and its forebears), the Duke of Lancaster's Own Yeomanry, and the 14th/20th King's Hussars — but also of the county itself from the twelfth century, when its name, 'Lancastria', first appears in the written record. The

Lancashire County and Regimental Museum, Preston.

military displays are more interesting than most, with reconstructions of scenes ranging from a First World War trench to a Victorian officers' mess. Some of the other displays highlight the services which the county council provides: one can sit at a Victorian teacher's desk or lie on the bed in a prison cell. Admission is free.

RAWTENSTALL
Rossendale Museum, Whitaker Park, Haslingden Road, Rawtenstall, Rossendale BB4 6RE. Telephone: 0706 217777 or 226509.

Housed in what used to be the home of the owner of New Hall Hey Mill, which stands with its graceful chimney in the bottom of the valley, the museum contains interesting displays on the history of Rossendale, its people and its industries, including a collection of toll boards from several local turnpike tollhouses. Admission is free.

RIBCHESTER
Ribchester Independent Museum of Roman Antiquities, Riverside, Ribchester, Preston PR3 3XS. Telephone: 025484 261.

Housed in a special building, opened in 1915, right in the middle of the Roman fort, the museum's displays explain the varied aspects of the life of Ribchester's Roman garrison and the extensive attached settlement, by means of coins, pottery, jewellery and inscriptions found in the vicinity. Also on show are the foundations of the fort's granaries and a facsimile of the magnificent bronze parade helmet which was found here in 1795. The original is in the British Museum.

Ribchester Museum of Childhood, 33 Church Street, Ribchester, Preston PR3 3YE. Telephone: 025484 520.

Attached to a toy shop with a wide variety of traditional and some modern gifts, this small privately run museum houses a large collection built up over the years by the owners. There are toys, trains, lead soldiers, dolls in all shapes, sizes and costumes, over fifty dolls' houses and model shops, a flea circus with a video of performing fleas and a twenty-piece working model fairground — an Aladdin's cave for children.

7
Lancashire's industrial heritage

The 'industrial revolution' is a shorthand term for the series of events between roughly 1750 and 1850 when technological advances in the textile industries and in engineering, accompanied by more efficient coal mining and improved means of transport, completely transformed the economy and society, first of Britain and then of most of the rest of the world. Lancashire was one of the cradles of the industrial revolution and still has many tangible reminders of that period.

Accrington: Railway Viaduct (OS 103: SD 758288). West of the town centre.

This is the most impressive of the several stone viaducts on the former East Lancashire Railway. Built on a sweeping curve of nineteen arches, it carries the line 60 feet (18 metres) above the river Hyndburn.

Anglezarke: Lead Mines Clough (OS 109: SD 630165). A mile or so north of Rivington and accessible along a path from Alance Bridge at the north-east corner of Yarrow Reservoir (OS 109: SD 627160).

Lead sulphide (or galena), from which lead was extracted by smelting, was mined intermittently on the Anglezarke Moors between 1692 and 1837. The remains of the workings in Lead Mines Clough have been partially excavated and restored; the most striking feature is the pit in which a waterwheel turned to drive machinery to pump out water from the mines and to crush the mixture of clays, galena and other minerals which had been extracted. A trail guide is available from the Great Barn information centre at Rivington (see chapter 2).

Barrowford: Tollhouse (OS 103: SD 862398).

Originally built in 1803 at the junction of the Marsden to Gisburn turnpike (A682) and the branch road to Colne (B6247), this tollhouse is now part of the Pendle Heritage Centre (see chapter 6). Between its upper windows is a painted board which indicates the tolls that had to be paid. There are others in the Rossendale Museum at Rawtenstall (see chapter 6).

Blackburn: Eanam Wharf, Eanam. (OS 103: SD 688282). Just off A677.

The Leeds and Liverpool Canal reached Blackburn from Accrington in 1810, and the wharf was built then and remains impressively complete with its tall warehouses and their overhanging canopies. The office block is a single-storey building with rounded ends right against the main road, which used to pass through the site, and the wharfmaster's house is at the west. The nearby Packet House pub is a reminder that, though most canal boats carried goods, there were also regular passenger services before the coming of the railways.

Blackburn: Ewood Aqueduct (OS 103: SD 676264). Just north of the junction of B6477 and A666.

This is the most impressive aqueduct on the Leeds and Liverpool Canal, a massive single arch of rusticated masonry, built in about 1815 to carry the canal over both the river Darwen and a road.

Burnley: Canal Embankment (OS 103: SD 844325).

One of the wonders of the English canal system, this was completed in 1796 to carry the Leeds and Liverpool Canal across the valley of the river Calder. Known locally as the 'Straight Mile', it really measures only three-quarters of a mile (1150 metres), but it is up to 60 feet (18 metres) high and contains more than 300,000 cubic yards of material, some from Gannow Tunnel.

The Tollhouse, Barrowford.

39

Burnley: Manchester Road Wharf (OS 103: SD 838323).

When the embankment (described above) was completed, the canal could be opened from Leeds to Burnley, and the Manchester Road Wharf was built as a terminus. It therefore had a tollhouse, which now accommodates a small museum (see chapter 6), as well as a warehouse. The earliest part of this — next to the tollhouse — was modelled on a contemporary barn and then greatly extended in the nineteenth century with a projecting canopy and iron cranes. A ten-minute walk on the towpath between the Manchester Road Wharf and Westgate leads through the area nicknamed the 'Weavers' Triangle', whose landscape of mid nineteenth-century mills and chimneys reflected in the canal is very evocative, apart from the lack of smoke, of Victorian times when Burnley was the cotton-weaving capital of the world. Another ten minutes' walk along the towpath will bring one to Gannow Tunnel. As at Foulridge Tunnel (see below) there is no towpath, and the boats had to be 'legged' through; the path over which the horses were meanwhile led can be seen to the right.

Industry recollected in tranquillity on the canal at Burnley.

Calder Vale: Mill and Mill Village (OS 102: SD 533458). 2 miles east of Garstang.

The mill is the best surviving example in Lancashire of a formerly water-powered mill; its pond and race can still be seen during an attractive short walk up the Calder valley. The mill opened in 1835, with housing for key workers in Long Row (which may have been built back-to-back) and, later, in the Victoria and Albert Terraces on the other side of the valley.

Chorley: Johnson's Hillock Locks (OS 102: SD 591206). Just off the minor road between Wheelton and Whittle-le-Woods.

Here is the canal junction where the Leeds and Liverpool met the Lancaster Canal. The original plan had foreseen that the Lancaster should link with the Leeds and Liverpool to get to the coal mines of Wigan, but the Lancaster was completed through to Wigan by 1803, when the canal from Leeds had got no further than Accrington! Finally, in 1816 this long curving sequence of seven locks had to be built to enable the Leeds and Liverpool to reach Wigan along the waters of the Lancaster canal.

Darwen: India Mill Chimney (OS 103: SD 693217). Just east of A666, a mile south of the town centre.

Hardly beautiful, but certainly unforgettable, this 300 feet (90 metres) high square chimney, built of brick on a rough stone base, was completed in 1867 and detailed to look like an Italian bell-tower.

Darwen: Mill Engine (OS 103: SD 693217). On A666 outside India Mill.

This well displayed 450 horsepower cross-compound steam engine was built in 1905. Its 16 foot (5 metre) flywheel, which rotated between the smaller, high-pressure cylinder and the larger, low-pressure one, is grooved to carry the ropes which once transmitted its power to the mill machinery. A few yards to the north, on the same side of the main road is a rotary calico-printing press.

Dunsop Bridge: Guide Post (OS 103: SD 657499). Where the road to Lancaster over the Trough of Bowland leaves the Slaidburn road.

The West Riding magistrates made an order in 1738 that posts should be erected at important road junctions to show the distances to the nearest market towns. This one was placed here as early as 1739 — it bears the date — and was later used as a base for a wrought iron guide post.

Fleetwood: Lighthouses (OS 102: SD 338485 and 339482).

The port of Fleetwood, the first new town of

A cross-compound mill engine at Darwen.

The Lower Lighthouse at Fleetwood.

The lighthouse at Glasson Dock.

the railway age, was opened in 1840 at the mouth of the river Wyre. The pretty white lighthouse on the shore and the tall pink one, called the Pharos, in the town were both designed by Decimus Burton and built, originally with gas lights, to guide ships in along the Wyre channel.

Foulridge: Canal Tunnel and Wharf (OS 103: SD 888425). Just north of B6251.

Near the wharf, with its barn-like warehouse, Foulridge Tunnel was opened in 1796, having taken five years to build. At just under a mile (1500 metres), it is the longest canal tunnel in Lancashire, but it has no towpath, so barges had to be 'legged' through, with the boatmen lying on their sides and, as it were, walking along the tunnel walls.

Galgate: Former Silk Mills and Mill Village (OS 102: SD 485557).

This fascinating group of stone-built mills, dating from 1792 and 1830 and originally water-powered, together with a brick-built mill dated 1852 whose steam engine later powered the whole complex, can easily be inspected because several floors are now retail showrooms. Along the same street there are a

The Lune Aqueduct, Lancaster.

number of two-storey cottages, but the village was extended on the turnpike (A6) with taller houses when the mill was enlarged.

Garstang: Tollhouse and Turnpike Milestones. Tollhouse at the junction of A6 and B6430 (OS 102: SD 490466).

This stone-built tollhouse probably dates from the 1820s, when parts of the turnpike from Garstang to Lancaster and beyond were realigned — the old road snakes from side to side of the present A6. The tollhouse is more than usually interesting because the posts for the tollgate, which was normally kept closed, still exist on either side of the road (B6430). North and south of Garstang on the A6 are the finest series of turnpike milestones in the county: to the south round-faced stones with cursive letters dating from the 1750s, and to the north triangular stones with Roman lettering associated with the realignments of the 1820s.

Glasson Dock: Port and Canal Basin (OS 102: SD 444562). 5 miles south-west of Lancaster, off A588.

The first wet dock in the present county was opened in 1791 to accommodate sea-going boats which could not attempt the passage up the treacherous river Lune to Lancaster, and its modernised lock gates still open at high tide. The tiny, original lighthouse is still to be seen, as is the link to the Lancaster Canal, which was made in 1825 through a large basin which is now a marina.

Lancaster: Lune Aqueduct (OS 97: SD 484638). Visible from A683 1 mile north of the city centre.

This is the finest masonry aqueduct in the United Kingdom. It was designed by John Rennie to leap boldly over the Lune on five semi-circular arches, carrying the Lancaster Canal 60 feet (18 metres) above the river. Because of its sober magnificence and scale — the stones which form the arches are 3 feet (90 cm) high — it has been a tourist attraction ever since it was completed in 1797, but the laconic inscription on the upstream side — TO PUBLIC PROSPERITY — declares its original purpose.

Lancaster: St George's Quay (OS 97: SD 473622).

Built soon after an Act of Parliament in 1749 allowed the formation of a port commission to improve the town's port facilities, the quay still retains several gaunt warehouses and, in the centre, the Custom House of 1764, which was designed by Richard Gillow, who was more famous for his furniture. It is one of the most elegant buildings in the county and now houses a fascinating Maritime Museum (see chapter 6).

Rawtenstall: Weavers' Cottages, Fall Barn Fold, off Bacup Road (OS 103: SD 815227).

The Weavers' Cottages are not cottages but the best surviving example in Lancashire of a late eighteenth-century loomshop. This was a sort of early factory, providing working space for handloom weavers on the two well lit upper floors, with living quarters, now demolished, behind them. As such it was intermediate between cottage industry and factory production.

Sunderland Point (OS 102: SD 426559). 5 miles south of Morecambe.

Not always accessible, because the road from Overton is cut twice daily by the tides, Sunderland Point has the earliest surviving remains of a port in Lancashire. Feeling that the port facilities in Lancaster were inadequate, the merchant Robert Lawson, who lived at Sunderland Hall in the early eighteenth century, built some warehouses and a small quay where goods could be unloaded for transport by cart to Lancaster. The quay was too exposed and the road to Lancaster was inconvenient, and so Sunderland Point was soon superseded by a quay at Glasson on the other bank of the Lune (see above). A single Georgian gate-pier now stands like a memorial at Sunderland on the deserted quay.

On the seashore, as distinct from the riverbank, lies another monument, called Sambo's Grave, with a brass inscription dated 1796. Nobody knows who Sambo was — probably a black servant to a ship's captain — but there are nearly always flowers on the grave.

Thornton: Marsh Mill (OS 102: SD 335425). On B5266.

Named and dated 1794 and built to the design of the Fylde's most famous millwright, Ralph Slater, this tower windmill is complete with all its machinery. Its sails and the fantail, which by spinning drives a mechanism to keep them facing the wind, have been restored to working order, and the mill is open to the public.

Whalley: Viaduct (OS 103: SD 727361).

Opened in 1850 to carry the Blackburn to Clitheroe railway line across the wide valley of the Calder, Whalley Viaduct is a major landscape feature: with a length of more than 600 yards (550 metres) and 48 arches, built of seven million bricks and rising to a height of 70 feet (21 metres) above the river, it is visible for miles around, a symbol of the railway engineer's confidence that he could overcome all natural obstacles. And yet, where it crosses the lane to Whalley Abbey (see chapter 3), the flanking arches have been given Gothic details to harmonise with the nearby fourteenth-century gatehouse.

Worsthorne: Shedden Limestone Hushings (OS 103: SD 894296). Best approached from the car park at SD 893288 on the Long Causeway, the old road between Burnley and Hebden Bridge.

These hushings are the strangest early industrial site in the county. Here limestone boulders were extracted from the sands and clays deposited during the ice ages by glaciers coming from the Craven area. Limestone was important for making mortar and for sweetening the acidic upland soils, and before the coming of the canal to Burnley in 1796 the best way of obtaining limestone was to wash away the surrounding glacial debris, a process called 'hushing': water from the moor tops was channelled into ponds, from which it was released in a controlled manner to swill away the unwanted sands and clays. Some remains of the dams and channels are visible today, and one of the kilns in which the limestone boulders were burnt has been rebuilt. A trail to explain the site has been devised, and a guide leaflet can be obtained from local tourist information centres.

The Arcade at Accrington.

8
Towns and villages

ABBEYSTEAD

Nestling in the well wooded valley of the river Wyre, the village of Abbeystead owes its romantic attractiveness as much to its setting as to its buildings. Its name derives from the fact that shortly before 1200 monks from Furness Abbey arrived here to establish a monastery, but they found the climate too harsh and moved to Ireland. A few of the houses date from the seventeenth century, but most were built in the traditional style in the late nineteenth century after the estate had been bought by the Earl of Sefton.

ACCRINGTON

Early closing Wednesday; market daily except Wednesday and Sunday.

Accrington is best known for its hard red bricks but is largely a stone-built town. It developed in the late eighteenth century on a fairly regular plan around the crossing point of two turnpikes; before then there had been little more than a scatter of houses for colliers and farmer-weavers on the northern flanks of the Rossendale moors. The coming of the Leeds and Liverpool Canal in 1801 and then of the railway in 1847 encouraged its development as an industrial centre, and indeed the nineteen-arch viaduct (see chapter 7) is the dominant feature of the town centre. St James's church in its attractive churchyard

dates originally from 1763. Nearby are the delicate glass-roofed Arcade of 1880, the wide-spanned Market Hall of 1868 and, with its imposing Corinthian portico, the Town Hall which was built in 1853 as a public hall, newsroom and mechanics' institute in honour of the Peel family, who were the largest employers in the area. The Haworth Art Gallery on Manchester Road is worth a visit (see chapter 6).

2 miles (3 km) to the west lies **Oswaldtwistle,** where the Stanhill post office was the home of James Hargreaves, who invented the spinning jenny in 1764. To the south of both towns rises Oswaldtwistle Moor, where there are good views northwards from the A677 over the Calder and Ribble valleys, and where Holdings' Country Pottery, opened in 1859 and still in production, can be visited.

ARKHOLME

This pretty village, largely composed of cottages dating from the seventeenth and eighteenth centuries with mullioned windows, straggles on either side of a road which leads down to a ford over the Lune. This was guarded by a motte and bailey castle, in whose bailey the late medieval parish church now stands.

About 3 miles (5 km) to the north stands the

village of **Whittington** with a winding street bordered by old cottages with highly decorative lintels, and a church which is also built next to the mound of a motte and bailey castle.

BACUP
Early closing Tuesday; market days Wednesday and Saturday.
Surrounded by hills in the upper valley of the Irwell, not far from its source on Deerplay Moor, the small mill town of Bacup is, at 827 feet (250 metres), the highest town in Lancashire. It contains what is claimed to be the shortest street in the world: Elgin Street, off the Market Place, which is only 17 feet (5 metres) long. The museum of the Natural History Society is open on Thursday evenings.

BARNOLDSWICK
Barnoldswick was in Yorkshire until 1974. It is normally approached from the A56 along a straight road which was built in the 1930s when Rolls-Royce established itself in Barnoldswick, which was then no more than a small cotton-weaving town. (The B in the names of such jet engines as the RB211 stands for Barnoldswick.) The medieval church of St Mary-le-Gill stands quite near to Greenber Field Locks, which mark the eastern end of the summit level of the Leeds and Liverpool Canal; at the other end of the town is the working steam engine at Bancroft Mill (see chapter 6).

BARROWFORD
The large village of Barrowford is well known locally for its locks and canal reservoirs and more widely as the home of the Pendle Heritage Centre (see chapter 6) in Park Hill, one of several late seventeenth-century houses. Nearby is the high-arched packhorse bridge at Higherford.

BELMONT
The nucleus of the present village is the mill village established around 1800 by the owners of the nearby bleaching and dyeing works, just off the old road from Bolton to Preston which was turnpiked in 1801. A pretty row of cottages, called Maria Place, is dated 1804. In the early nineteenth century reservoirs were built here to supply pure water to the people of Bolton. The church of St Peter stands by an attractive small lake on the road over the moors to Rivington.

BLACKBURN
Early closing Thursday; market daily.
Blackburn was an old-established market town in the valley of the Blakewater which became a cotton-manufacturing centre in the late eighteenth century, specialising in weaving in the late nineteenth century. It is now also the home of three large breweries. Its importance as an industrial centre developed after the arrival of the Leeds and Liverpool Canal at Eanam Wharf (see chapter 7) in 1810, and its fine Gothic-style Cotton Exchange with its polygonal entrance hall (now the foyer of a cinema opposite the Town Hall) was opened in 1865. Two other noteworthy reminders of the cotton industry can be seen nearby — the Lewis Museum of Textile Machinery (see chapter 6) and the Hart Collection of coins and illustrated manuscripts in the Blackburn Museum (see chapter 6); both were given by local industrialists.

The town centre was rebuilt in the 1960s and 1970s, in a much more attractive manner than one usually finds. Just to the south stands the Anglican cathedral (see chapter 4) in an extensive churchyard, while just to the north are two other reminders of the town's pre-industrial past: the well proportioned, brick-built Richmond Terrace, which was completed in 1838, and the elegant St John's church, of 1789, with its domed tower.

Blackpool Tower.

Blackburn has a modern water fun centre, just to the west of the town centre, called Waves; it has a 200 feet (60 metres) long water flume, a wave machine, waterfall and three 100-year-old palm trees. The town is well endowed with parks: Corporation Park along Preston New Road is probably the most attractive, while along Preston Old Road is the more extensive Witton Country Park (see chapter 2).

BLACKPOOL
Early closing Wednesday.

Blackpool is a place of superlatives, unique and second to none: the largest town in the present county of Lancashire, it contains in the Pleasure Beach the biggest tourist attraction in Britain, which draws some 6,500,000 visitors per year; for three-quarters of a century the Tower, at 518 feet (158 metres), was the tallest structure in the United Kingdom, while its promenade from the low cliffs in the north to the sandhills in the south stretches for no less than 7 miles (11 km), a distance which can be doubled if one includes the total length from Fleetwood to Lytham; along the northern two-thirds, from Starr Gate to Fleetwood, runs the electric tram system which, when it was opened in 1885, was the first in Britain and is now the only one.

The first modest hotels were built in the late eighteenth century, but the town hardly grew before the coming of the railway in 1846. The building of the three piers between 1863 and 1893 and of the glass-domed Winter Garden in 1875-8 led to a boom in the 1890s, symbolised by the erection of the Tower in 1894. But Blackpool has never stood still and prides itself on its vitality and search for novelty, typified by the changing themes of the Illuminations which extend the season into September and October.

One does not go to Blackpool to look at old buildings, but the Tower Ballroom and the Grand Theatre, both designed by Frank Matcham in the 1890s, are worth a visit to see the rococo richness of their gilded plasterwork and painted ceilings. One goes to Blackpool to enjoy oneself and there is no lack of opportunity: several venues offer both to families and others a complete day out. Along the Golden Mile behind the sands of the South Shore are the Tower with its aquarium, its ballroom and its circus, the Sandcastle with its leisure pools, wave pools, water slides, games rooms and constant summer temperatures, and the Pleasure Beach, which claims to have more exciting fun rides than anywhere in the world. Inland there are the 254 acre (110 ha) Stanley Park and the Zoo — the most modern in Europe with five hundred animals, of both familiar and little-known species.

BOLTON-LE-SANDS

Bolton-le-Sands stands just off the A6 above the meandering line of the Lancaster Canal. The church has a western tower typical of the late fifteenth century; there are pleasant views across Morecambe Bay from the churchyard, while the street called The Nook (just to the north-east) has three or four small houses dating from around 1700. One mile (2 km) to the south, at **Slyne**, the Manor House is an attractive symmetrical house with cross-windows and a decorative lintel dated 1681, while one mile (2 km) to the south-west **Hest Bank** is the traditional starting point of the 'road' across the sands of Morecambe Bay to the Furness area (see chapter 2).

BURNLEY
Early closing Tuesday; market daily except Tuesday.

First established near the confluence of the Brun and the Calder, Burnley is a town surrounded by hills: every approach is downhill, and the views from the moorland roads from Bacup and Rawtenstall are particularly fine, with Pendle Hill as a backdrop.

Like Blackburn, Burnley has been a market town since the middle ages and developed as a centre of cotton manufacturing and coal mining after the coming of the Leeds and Liverpool Canal in 1796 and then of the railway in 1848. (In the late nineteenth century it claimed to be the cotton-weaving capital of the world.) For this reason it shows better than anywhere else in Lancashire the impact of the industrial revolution on a traditional market town. The canal from Leeds arrived at the Manchester Road Wharf (see chapter 7) after running along an enormous embankment to the east of the town; the railway passes to the west of the town on a newly cleaned viaduct of fifteen arches. To the west of the wharf is the area nicknamed the Weavers' Triangle, where a number of mill chimneys can still be seen mirrored in the waters of the canal. The canal tollhouse is now the Weavers' Triangle Visitor Centre (see chapter 6).

Much of the town centre has been developed rather badly since the Second World War, but there are visible reminders of Burnley's Victorian prosperity in the Town Hall on Manchester Road, several nearby banks and the fine former Mechanics' Institute (next to the Town Hall), which is now an entertainments centre. What is more surprising is the number of good classical buildings from the inter-war period just to the east of Manchester Road — the Library, the former headquarters of the Burnley Building Society next door and the Magistrates' Court on the opposite side of the square. In the northern suburbs of Burnley is Harle Syke, home of the Queen Street Mill (see chapter 6), while to the east Towneley

Hall, the town's museum in a fine country house, is also well worth visiting (see chapter 5).

CARNFORTH
Early closing Thursday.

Carnforth developed in Victorian times around an ironworks built near an important railway junction. It is now most famous as the home of the working railway museum called Steamtown (see chapter 6) but also has one of the best second-hand bookshops in the county. One mile (2 km) to the north is the Pine Lake water-sport centre (see chapter 2) and beyond that the pretty village of **Borwick**, whose green is dominated by the gables and battlements of Borwick Hall (occasionally open), which was built in the late sixteenth century around a medieval pele tower.

CATON

Now a suburb of Lancaster, Caton stands just upstream of the beautiful, well wooded Crook o' Lune, where, towards the end of the ice ages, the river cut a winding channel through the high ground between its middle reaches and its estuary. The original village was at Brookhouse, where the church of St Paul, with its blocked Norman doorway, stands within a huddle of old houses, but during the eighteenth century the village centre moved westward down to the new line of the Lancaster to Richmond turnpike and the valleys of Artle Beck and Forge Beck, where a number of mills were built.

The road from Caton towards the Trough of Bowland road runs through the very attractive Quernmore valley; now used by the little river Conder, this was an earlier course of the river Lune.

CHIPPING

The name of Chipping suggests that it was once a market centre serving the valleys of the Loud and the Hodder, and this idea of earlier importance is borne out by a medieval church (of some interest) and a number of well built late seventeenth-century houses with mullioned windows: the Post Office, dated 1668, and Brabyn's School, dated 1684, are the best examples. Just north of the village there is a furniture factory, originally powered by water; the stream now turns the waterwheel of a restaurant in the village, which used to be a corn mill.

CHORLEY
Early closing Wednesday; market days Tuesday, Friday and Saturday.

Standing at the southern end of the Central Lancashire new town, Chorley is an old-established market town. Its most attractive features are the two municipal parks at Dux-

bury and at Astley, where the Hall (see chapter 5) is well worth a visit. To the north-east is the canal junction at Johnson's Hillock (see chapter 7), while 4 miles (6 km) to the south-west, near Charnock Richard, is the Magical Kingdom of Camelot, a theme park designed especially for children, with medieval jousting, the wizard Merlin in his grotto and a 'petting zoo' as well as the usual thrill rides.

CLITHEROE
Early closing Wednesday; market days Tuesday and Saturday.

Clitheroe is probably the most attractive small town in Lancashire, its industrial past and present overshadowed by the traditional appearance of a market town established at the gateway of a castle. Its main street winds gently down and then up along a low ridge linking the hills on which stand the castle (see chapter 3) and St Mary's church, which was largely designed by Thomas Rickman in 1828. There are no outstandingly fine buildings, but no ugly ones either, and the round tower of the library is a pleasing focal point in the view. Up

The Local History Museum at Colne.

47

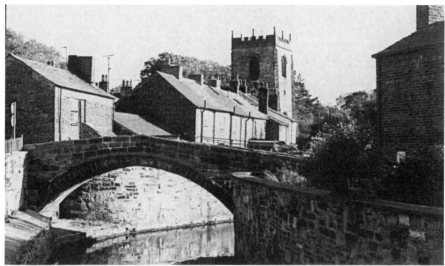

Croston church and bridge.

to its left are Rickman's Town Hall (into which the library now extends) and several other late Georgian houses.

To the east of the town the great whale-backed hill of Pendle dominates the skyline, while to the north are the tall chimneys of a cement works which makes use of the local limestone; the former quarry at Salthill nearby is the site of an interesting geology trail, best visited after the museum (see chapter 6).

Around Clitheroe there are several attractive old villages, including **Pendleton** (just off the road to the Nick o' Pendle), which lies very prettily on either side of a brook, railed off to prevent accidents, and **Waddington.** Here a stream runs through a garden along the main street, which climbs past an attractive, largely medieval church to Waddington Fell, from where there are fine views down the Ribble valley and across to Pendle and the Rossendale hills.

COLNE
Early closing Tuesday; market daily except Tuesday and Sunday.

At the end of the railway line from Preston, the main street of Colne, Albert Road, runs past the memorial to Wallace Hartley, the bandmaster on the *Titanic*, and along a windy ridge between two valleys, once lined by cotton-weaving sheds. The town's origins go back much further than the nineteenth century, however — unlike those of neighbouring Nelson — and the church of St Bartholomew (which contains some attractive Georgian memorials) is medieval. The former grammar

school, built in 1812 to the east of the churchyard, now houses a small local history museum which is part of the Pendle Heritage Centre. There is also a museum about the British in India, with coins, medals, uniforms and model soldiers, photographs and a working model of the railway from Kalka to Simla.

CROSTON
At first sight Croston is no more than a commuter suburb with a little light industry, but the old village centre around the church is much more attractive. The church, with its leaning fifteenth-century tower and wide-spreading roof which covers both the nave and the aisles, is approached down a cobbled lane lined with old brick cottages. To the west of the churchyard is the village school (rebuilt in 1827), which backs on to the river Yarrow, while to the east one can glimpse the former rectory, which is dated 1722 and has an elegant bowed front and pretty curved gables. Back on the main street, one should turn left for the narrow, hump-backed Town Bridge (dated 1682) or right to see the picturesque ruins of the Georgian Gothick gateway to the rectory.

DARWEN
Early closing Tuesday; market daily.

The best approach to Darwen is by rail from Bolton, for this enables one to appreciate how it clings to the hillsides of the narrow valley of the river which gives the town its name. The pre-industrial village was on the east side of the valley, but the town developed rapidly during the nineteenth century with a line of mills — producing cotton at first but later paper — strung out along the Blackburn turnpike (now the A666). The finest mill of all is India Mill (see chapter 7). To the west of the town is the Jubilee Tower, from which there is a very fine view. It was built in 1898 to celebrate both Queen Victoria's diamond jubilee and also the right of Darwen people to have unrestricted access to Darwen Moor.

DOWNHAM

One of the prettiest villages in Lancashire, Downham is best seen from up by the church; here the view extends over its houses, built of the local limestone and scattered around an open green, with a stream and a bridge at the bottom and Pendle Hill in the background. We owe the unspoilt beauty of the setting and the houses to the fact that the whole village is owned by Lord Clitheroe, who controls developments very strictly and whose grandfather paid for the electricity supply cables to be laid underground in the 1930s.

EARBY

Like its neighbour, Barnoldswick, Earby is a small textile town which used to be in Yorkshire. It is now best known for its Lead Mines Museum, housed in the Old Grammar School. This contains varied artefacts, old photographs, a large collection of mineral samples and working models relating to lead mining in the Pennine Dales.

FLEETWOOD

Early closing Wednesday; market days Tuesday and Friday, also Saturday from July to October.

Fleetwood was the first port of the railway age, the brainchild of the local squire, Sir Peter Hesketh-Fleetwood of Rossall, who planned to develop a seaside resort and port on his estate at the mouth of the river Wyre and got the architect Decimus Burton to design the layout of the town and some of its buildings. Sir Peter's money ran out before his dream was fulfilled, but Burton's plan and some of his buildings — notably the two lighthouses (see chapter 7), the North Euston Hotel and Queen's Terrace — can still be seen. Fleetwood became a fishing port (whose story is traced in the museum: see chapter 6) but since the 'Cod War' of 1976 it has developed a new role, with scheduled vehicle ferry services to Ireland.

The town is still a seaside resort, with a boating pool and swimming bath — because the sea retreats a long way at low tide — and fine views from the Mount across Morecambe Bay to the Lakeland hills and those of the Forest of Bowland. A popular trip is to come on the tram from Blackpool, visit the market and then cross the Wyre by the ferry to Knott End.

GARSTANG

Early closing Wednesday; market day Thursday.

Garstang is a small market town which grew up where Lancashire's great north-south main road crosses the Wyre. 200 yards (180 metres) to the west the river on an elegant aqueduct, designed by the engineer John Rennie. The market cross, an eighteenth-century column on a medieval stepped base, stands outside the Royal Oak Hotel, while the former town hall, an attractive Georgian brick building of 1755 whose arcaded lower storey once sheltered market traders, is on the other side of the street. The tollhouse and turnpike milestones are described in chapter 7.

Garstang Town Hall.

2 miles (4 km) to the north lies the pretty village of **Scorton**, whose houses cluster loosely around the entrance to the wooded park of Wyresdale Hall.

GISBURN

Gisburn, which used to be in Yorkshire until 1974, is an attractive small town with a wide main street, where every view includes an enormous tree in the graveyard of a pleasant medieval church. Of several old houses perhaps the most interesting is what is now the Ribblesdale Arms hotel. An inscription over the door informs us that Thomas Lister built the house in 1635 and that it cost him £855 — no small sum. The pretty early-nineteenth-century Gothick lodges at the entrance to the drive of Gisburne Park are worth a short detour. The Gisburn Steam Museum is described in chapter 6.

GOOSNARGH

The old village centre stands to the north of the Broughton to Longridge road and comprises an attractive late medieval church, two public houses and a building called Bushell's Hospital. This was founded, in what had been his father's house (built in 1722), according to the will of the local parson, William Bushell (who died in 1735).

2 miles (3 km) to the north is the hamlet of **Inglewhite**, a pleasing scatter of houses around a large irregularly shaped green, with a market cross which marks the site of cattle and sheep fairs. Another 2 miles (3 km) to the north is the Beacon Fell Country Park (see chapter 2).

Gothick lodges at Gisburne Park.

GREAT HARWOOD
Early closing Tuesday; market day Friday.

Great Harwood was a market town long before it developed a small-scale cotton-weaving industry after the railway opened in 1877, and its Market Square on the hilltop is still more or less the centre of the place. The Town Hall, the neighbouring bank and the monument to John Mercer (who invented in 1850 a process, called 'mercerisation', which made it easier to print textiles) are an attractive ensemble from the early years of the twentieth century. To the north, the parish church of St Bartholomew is largely late medieval, while the Roman Catholic church of St Hubert, to the east, contains some very fine Victorian stained glass windows.

HASLINGDEN
Early closing Wednesday; market days Tuesday and Friday.

Pleasantly set in the hills between Rawtenstall and Accrington, Haslingden is a small textile town, now best known as the home of the Museum of the Lancashire Textile Industry at Helmshore (see chapter 6).

HEYSHAM
Early closing Wednesday.

Now part of Morecambe, but a place of considerably greater antiquity, Heysham is a town where the past, the present and the future co-exist strangely. The main street of the old village is a mixture of traditional cottages and seaside shops, but all the bustle is left behind immediately one enters St Peter's

Bushell's Hospital, Goosnargh.

churchyard (see chapter 4). On the cliffs above stand the ruins of St Patrick's Chapel (see chapter 3), and the view from here stretches out northward over Morecambe Bay to the Lakeland hills. To the west, however, one sees first of all the busy Heysham Harbour, opened by the Midland Railway in 1904 and now the supply base for the Morecambe Bay gasfield; beyond and behind that there rise the massive cubic reactor houses of Heysham's two nuclear power stations. A tower has been built just off the road to the power stations to allow people to observe the site and read an explanation of how nuclear power is used to generate electricity.

HORNBY

Hornby has two castles, a motte and bailey (see chapter 3) down by the Loyne Bridge, and one in its own grounds which was extended during the nineteenth century around a medieval pele tower. It looks particularly fine from the Wenning bridge on Main Street, from where there is an extensive view down the Lune valley. Main Street is wide and straight and leads past several eighteenth-century cottages to the parish church of St Margaret with its notable octagonal tower (see chapter 4).

A mile or so to the north-west, across the Lune, is the pretty village of **Gressingham**, where few cottages can be seen from a single spot because of the steeply sloping site and well treed gardens. The church was largely

rebuilt in 1734 but has a fine late Norman doorway.

2 miles (3 km) to the south-east is the village of **Wray**, a fine collection of cottages and farmhouses dating from the seventeenth and eighteenth centuries, set at the junction of roads leading through the wooded valleys of the Roeburn and the Hindburn to the open fells above.

HURSTWOOD

The hamlet of Hurstwood nestles in a tree-fringed hollow on the edge of the moors at the end of the road from the mill village of Worsthorne. Most people come here for the walks on the wide open hills which link Lancashire and Yorkshire and are dotted with prehistoric earthworks and burial sites, but the houses and their barns are well worth a second look. Hurstwood Hall with its gables and mullioned windows is dated 1579; Spenser House is even more attractive and may have been the home for two years of the Elizabethan poet Edmund Spenser. One can also walk to the limestone hushings on Worsthorne Moor (see chapter 7) from Hurstwood.

KIRKHAM

Early closing Wednesday.

Kirkham is the old market town of the southern half of the Fylde, and the circle of fishstones, surmounted by an old street-lamp, still survives in the Market Square, opposite

51

The Market Square at Great Harwood.

one of the town's two fine Georgian houses; the other is at the top of the hill a little way to the east. Three of the town's churches have spires, but only the parish church of St Michael is worth a visit (see chapter 4).

2 miles (3 km) south-west lies **Wrea Green**, where the church with its spire is a pleasing backdrop to the large village green, which is graced by a duckpond in the north-west corner.

LANCASTER
Early closing Wednesday; market daily except Wednesday and Sunday.

Lancaster is the most attractive town in Lancashire and the most interesting for anyone with a liking for history, because it preserves significant reminders of most stages in its development. It is the only city in the present county and, though it is no longer the administrative centre, it is still the county town and proud of the fact that the Queen is the Duke of Lancaster.

The first feature in Lancaster which most people notice is the dome of the restored Ashton Memorial in Williamson Park (see chapter 6), but the best place to start a walk around the most interesting parts of the old town is on Castle Hill, where the story of the town begins too.

The castle (see chapter 3) was begun soon after the Norman Conquest to guard the lowest crossing place of the river Lune, just like the Roman fort which preceded it in AD 79. The great gatehouse, surrounded by the houses of Georgian gentry and merchants, was built for Henry IV, the Duke of Lancaster who usurped the throne in 1399; it is the first part of the castle which one sees but cannot be visited because it is part of the prison.

The Priory Church (see chapter 4) stands on the site of the county's first monastery, which was founded in 1094. The churchyard is the best place to appreciate Lancaster's setting, which invited both the Romans and the Normans to fortify this hill. On a clear day the view across the bay towards the Lakeland hills is very fine.

Lancaster stands on a tidal river and had a port of some consequence from medieval times; its golden age was the eighteenth century, when most of the town's finest buildings including Skerton Bridge, the most elegant in the county, were built. The best way to appreciate the port is to walk down to St George's Quay (see chapter 7) and back, to visit the much acclaimed Maritime Museum (see chapter 6) which has been established in Richard Gillow's Custom House. On the way down one can make a short detour to the right to see the remains of a Roman bath-house (see chapter 3).

Back at the church, one should walk towards the town centre down the two flights of steps (after first enjoying the view across the town). Just before one crosses the main road, one passes on the right the Judges' Lodging, the oldest house in the town and the home of another fine museum (see chapter 6).

Across the main road in Church Street there are two grand Georgian houses on the left. A little further on the right is Sun Street, where, at the end on the right, stands the Music Room (see chapter 6), which was built as a garden house in the 1730s.

Turning left at the end of Sun Street into Market Street, one finds on the left the Old Town Hall, which now houses the City Museum (see chapter 6).

Down Market Street, through the shopping precinct and across the southbound main road one comes to Dalton Square, which was laid out speculatively in a grid of surrounding streets by the Dalton family from nearby Thurnham Hall at the end of the eighteenth century. The area, which had been the site of a Dominican friary in the middle ages, was never fully developed, because the prosperity of Lancaster's port began to decline around 1800. The most striking buildings are therefore the opulent Town Hall and the impressive monument to Queen Victoria, which were given to his native town in 1909 by Lord Ashton, the millionaire king of the linoleum industry. Beneath the statue of the old queen are bronze bas-relief portraits of eminent Victorians.

It was Lord Ashton's father, James Williamson, who began in 1863 to lay out the park which bears his name as a means of giving employment to his workers during the 'cotton famine'. The memorial (see chapter 6) which his son built can be seen from Dalton Square; behind it on the Clitheroe road is the new Lancaster Leisure Park (which used to be the Hornsea Pottery). There is still a pottery shop, as well as a children's adventure playground and a 19 acre (8 ha) survival unit for rare breeds of farm animals. On the way up to them is the Roman Catholic cathedral (see chapter 4).

To the south of the town is the university, where visitors are welcome; it is laid out in attractive grounds, on a ridge which enjoys fine views, rather like an extended Oxbridge college with courtyards on either side of a traffic-free walkway.

LEYLAND
Early closing Wednesday; market days Tuesday, Friday and Saturday.

To most people the name of Leyland means buses and trucks, and these are appropriately commemorated and displayed in the town's celebrated British Commercial Vehicle Museum (see chapter 6). The town's history goes back however, to the middle ages, and the oldest buildings stand around the crossroads near the Market Place and St Andrew's church, in which a nineteenth-century nave

The Judges' Lodging, Lancaster.

Worden Hall, Leyland.

links a fourteenth-century chancel to a sixteenth-century tower. The graveyard too, behind its imposing wall, contains a large collection of interesting tombstones, as well as the old grammar school, which now houses a small museum of local history.

To the south of the crossroads lies Worden Park, where the Lancashire branch of the Council for the Protection of Rural England has its headquarters and its information and exhibition centre next to a collection of craft workshops in the stable block of the former hall.

LONGRIDGE
Early closing Wednesday; market day Thursday.

The little town of Longridge takes its name from the long sandstone hill which rises to a height of 1150 feet (350 metres) between the valleys of the Ribble and the Hodder. Now largely a commuter suburb, it was once famous for its quarries, now an enormous caravan site, and the fine Longridge sandstone can be seen, often used with brick, in many nineteenth-century buildings in central Lancashire. Longridge Fell itself is a pleasingly open area, especially on the higher parts where there are expanses of heathery moorland, and there are good views to be had from many parts, but notably from the road over Jeffrey Hill (see chapter 1).

The most interesting buildings in Longridge

itself are twenty cottages, called Club Row, on Higher Road (the minor road to Jeffrey Hill and Chipping) which were built between 1794 and 1804 by the members of a building society; they are thought to be the oldest such houses in Lancashire.

LYTHAM ST ANNE'S
Early closing Wednesday.

The borough of Lytham St Anne's (now part of the Fylde borough) was formed in 1922 by a marriage between Lytham, a township which was mentioned in the Domesday Book, and St Anne's, which was developed by an estate company around a church dedicated to St Anne in 1873. Lytham was laid out in an equally careful way at the end of the eighteenth century and during the nineteenth by the Clifton family of Lytham Hall.

The purpose of the amalgamation of the two townships was to prevent their being swallowed separately by Blackpool, and to this day they are more residential towns than seaside resorts. However, St Anne's does have a short pier, and Lytham has what is called the Beach — a very attractive open expanse of grass with a pretty windmill with a full set of sails and a fantail — from where there are views to the hills of the West Pennine Moors. Between the two townships there is a large boating lake at Fairhaven, where one can even sail dinghies, but the most famous amenity is the Royal Lytham St Anne's Golf Club, which is one of the venues for the British Open Championship. The Motive Power Museum at Lytham is described in chapter 6.

MELLING

Melling is the prettiest village on the east bank of the Lune — a long cluster of old stone houses with mullioned windows jutting at odd angles into the narrow and winding main road. Almost every one is worth a second look, but one must beware of the traffic. The safest viewpoint is the graveyard of St Wilfred's church, which in its present form dates from the late fifteenth century; since it is built on a steeply sloping hillside, the floor in the chancel is more than 5 feet (1.5 metres) higher than that of the nave. The finest house in the village is the hotel standing by the junction of the main road with the road to Wennington (look out for the old guidepost with fingers but no distances); it was built as Melling Hall in the early eighteenth century with five windows across the front, but towards the end of the century it was refronted with an attractive porch with Ionic columns and only three windows in the lower storeys.

MORECAMBE

Early closing Wednesday; market days Tuesday and Thursday, also Friday between mid May and September.

'Beauty surrounds, health abounds' is the motto in the entrance to Morecambe Town Hall, which overlooks the bay from which the town took its name in 1870. The original fishing village, from which the resort began to develop in the early nineteenth century, had been called Poulton-le-Sands. It was only with the coming of the railway in 1850 that it grew significantly, and then, like Blackpool, it boomed in the 1880s and 1890s, catering especially for mill workers from Yorkshire — a tradition which still survives.

Morecambe has never been more than a distant rival of Blackpool, but it has comparable attractions like Frontierland, a western theme park with over thirty rides; the Superdome and Leisure Park with its heated open-air swimming pool, wave machine and water chute; the Illuminations along the Promenade and in Happy Mount Park from mid August until the end of October; and the Marineland Oceanarium with its performing sea-lions and dolphins, as well as alligators in a tropical aquarium. It also has amenities which Blackpool will never have: the changing views from the 4 mile (6 km) long Promenade across the bay to the Lakeland hills, with sunsets which inspired Turner and many lesser artists, safe sailing at high tide and, at low water, the presence of thousands of waders and other waterfowl.

NELSON

Early closing Tuesday; market daily except Tuesday and Sunday.

Nelson is a nineteenth-century cotton-weaving town which took its name from the Lord Nelson pub when the East Lancashire Railway opened its station nearby in 1849. The modern shopping centre does nothing for the townscape, but the old town centre on the western side of the A56 has a certain late Victorian period charm, as do the station and the Station Hotel, which dates from 1893. As always in north-east Lancashire, what the town lacks in beauty is provided by the landscape, and there are fine views from the municipal golf course (to the east), near which stands the prehistoric hillfort called Castercliff (see chapter 3).

NEWCHURCH IN PENDLE

Almost the first thing one sees in Newchurch are the 'witches' huddling outside a shop, for this — in folklore if not in fact — is

Lytham Mill.

the heart of the 'Pendle Witch Country'. The shortest ways up Pendle start from Barley, about 1 mile (2 km) to the north, while Roughlee Old Hall, the home of Alice Nutter, who was hanged as a witch in 1612, stands about 2 miles (3 km) away to the east. However, the best feature of Newchurch is its largely Georgian church (see chapter 4).

ORMSKIRK
Early closing Wednesday; market daily except Wednesday and Sunday.

From the sound of the name of the place, there was a church at Ormskirk before the Norman Conquest, and there is a twelfth-century window in the chancel of the parish church (see chapter 4). Ormskirk has been a market town since 1286 and now has an attractive pedestrianised centre. Few of its buildings are old, and the finest, apart from the parish church, is the house on the corner of Burscough Street and Derby Street which was built in the 1770s.

Since Ormskirk lies on the flat plain of west Lancashire, it gets its water not from reservoirs in the hills but from boreholes and stores it in water towers. The concrete mushroom on Scarth Hill to the east of the town is the most recent, while the elephantine tower just north of the town centre dates from 1850; it is the oldest in Lancashire and maybe in Britain.

OVERTON
The interest of this village is concentrated at the two extremities, for that is where the oldest cottages cluster around Georgian houses which are focal points in the view. Beyond the village to the south-east the quaint old church of St Helen, with its fine late Norman doorway, stands in its windswept churchyard looking over the Lune estuary to Glasson Dock (see chapter 7). To the south of Overton, and cut off twice a day by the tides, is the former port of Sunderland Point (see chapter 7).

PADIHAM
Early closing Tuesday.

Padiham developed as a small cotton-weaving town during the nineteenth century but is more attractive than most because of its hilly site, its winding main street and the fine tower of its parish church, opened in 1869. Some of the side streets too have pleasing terraces of houses, probably designed in the office of Sir Charles Barry, who was responsible for the remodelling of the superb Gawthorpe Hall (see chapter 5), which stands a mile to the east.

PARBOLD
Parbold is now largely composed of modern suburban housing. It developed originally —

presumably as an offshoot of the picturesque village of Newburgh, a mile to the west — around the canal wharf where the new Leeds and Liverpool Canal was linked in 1772 to the existing Douglas Navigation. One can still see the tower of an eighteenth-century windmill to the west of Station Road, and the original canal warehouse to the east. The canal junction stands just to the west of the narrow valley through which the river Douglas and the railway pass between the high ground of the Ashurst-Billinge ridge and Parbold Hill, from which there are fine views southwards over the Mersey Plain to the hills of North Wales.

PILLING
There used to be an old saying that Pilling Moss, like God's grace, was boundless. The fens have now been drained and the roads run in straight lengths above the level of the fertile black-earthed fields, which rise at Eagland Hill to 33 feet (10 metres)! The journey under the vast expanse of sky is more interesting than beautiful, perhaps, but is worth making for Pilling has two pleasing churches (see chapter 4) and, at Lane Ends on the new embankment which since 1983 has prevented the road to Lancaster from being flooded twice daily by the tide, an attractive belvedere from which one can look out over Cockerham Sands with their thousands of wading birds and then over Morecambe Bay to the Lakeland hills.

POULTON-LE-FYLDE
Early closing Wednesday.

So called to distinguish it from Poulton-le-Sands (which has become Morecambe), this Poulton has been for centuries the market town of the northern half of the Fylde and was also for a time its port. Skippool is now no more than a mooring place for yachts, but the pedestrianised Market Place survives with its cross — a seventeenth-century column on a medieval stepped base — its stocks, its whipping post and its fishstones. In the background is the interesting parish church of St Chad in its pleasant graveyard (see chapter 4).

3 miles (5 km) to the east is the pretty estate village of **Singleton,** with cottages of a similar design. Everything, including St Anne's church and a specially ornate shed for the fire engine, was built in the 1860s by the Miller family, who had made their money as cotton spinners in Preston.

PRESTON
Early closing Thursday; market daily except Sunday.

Preston refers to itself as Proud Preston and it has a good reason for its pride. In 1179 it became the first town in the county to receive a borough charter and in 1328 it was granted the right to hold a Guild Merchant, or trade

Padiham Town Hall.

St John's church, Preston.

fair, every twenty years. (The next one is due in 1992).

Since 1768 every one of its male inhabitants over 21 has had the right to vote in parliamentary elections. Since 1798 the town has been the administrative centre of the county and since 1888 the home of the county council. In 1816 Preston was the first town outside London to light its streets by gas, and in 1958 the much needed Preston bypass was the first stretch of motorway in Great Britain.

With its suburbs of Fulwood, Penwortham and Walton-le-Dale, Preston is the biggest town in the county and has one of the most modern shopping centres, but it has few reminders of its ancient past.

The town was established on a bluff above the lowest crossing place of the river Ribble and still presents a fine sight from the B6230 between Walton-le-Dale and Samlesbury — if one can imagine the view without the ungainly flats and office blocks. Preston became a town of spires during the nineteenth century, for, more than most towns in the county, it saw a

rivalry between Catholics and Anglicans which expressed itself in a sort of competition as to who could produce the finest steeple. The Catholics perhaps won with St Walburge's 300 foot (90 metre) finger of stone. The finest secular spire is the one which rises above the Crown Court, opened in 1903 as the County Sessions House. It is best seen from the Market Place, which is still the centre of the town. In its shadow, but by no means outfaced, stands the very fine Harris Museum and Art Gallery (see chapter 6).

Just south of the Market Place, Fishergate runs from west to east. To the east one passes St John's church, one of the most attractive Victorian Gothic churches in the county, with a beautiful steeple; it was built in 1855. Further down, and then turning right at the end of the road by the prison, one comes to the new and very worthwhile County and Regimental Museum (see chapter 6).

To the west along Fishergate and then to the south along Chapel Street one reaches the tree filled Winckley Square, late Georgian in character if not in every building. This is the introduction to a whole area of pleasant nineteenth-century streets, leading to the fine Avenham and Miller parks by the river.

To the west of Preston is **Penwortham,** with a pleasing medieval church and an overgrown castle mound, probably raised by Roger of Poitou, from which there is a fine view of Preston. To the north is **Fulwood,** where the barracks also house the Museum of the Loyal Regiment (see chapter 6), and to the north again are **Broughton** and **Woodplumpton** with their attractive churches.

RAWTENSTALL
Early closing Tuesday; market days Thursday and Saturday.

Rawtenstall developed during the nineteenth century from a number of small hamlets based on medieval cattle farms established on the edges of the uplands north and south of the Rossendale valley, through which the Irwell flows. To the north of the present main road (A681) through the town from Haslingden to Bacup the old road runs at a higher level between the original hamlets, giving good views over the town in the valley. At Waterfoot the valley becomes a narrow gorge, where the river and the turnpike left so little space that the railway engineers had to tunnel their way through. Early industry concentrated on woollen and then cotton weaving, but since about 1900 the making of shoes has been prominent. These industries are illustrated in the Weavers' Cottages and the Rossendale Museum (see chapters 7 and 6 respectively).

There are two fine Methodist chapels in Rawtenstall, Longholme in the centre and what is now the Old People's Centre by the big roundabout; built in 1842 and 1857, they show well the change in taste from restraint to opulence which occurred in the mid nineteenth century. 2 miles (3 km) to the north at Goodshaw is the Old Baptist Chapel (see chapter 4). For the sports enthusiast there is Ski Rossendale (see chapter 3) on the Haslingden Old Road, while for the teetotaller or the simply curious the last temperance bar in Britain, Herbal Health on Bank Street, will serve such traditional drinks as sarsaparilla or dandelion and burdock.

RIBCHESTER
The name of Ribchester suggests a Roman site and the visitor will not be disappointed, for the village stands around the site of a small fort which was built by Agricola in AD 79 to guard a ford over the Ribble (see chapter 3). Part of the ditch around the fort still surrounds the church of St Wilfrid (see chapter 4). A small museum (see chapter 6) on Riverside, from where there is a lovely view up the

Ribble valley to Pendle Hill, tells the story of the fort, and there are other Roman remains to be seen, notably a bath-house behind the White Bull pub. Just along Church Street is the Museum of Childhood (see chapter 6).

RIVINGTON
Rivington must be one of the prettiest villages in Lancashire, its stone houses scattered around a green on the edge of Lever Park (see chapter 2) and set between the hills of the West Pennine Moors and the beautiful reservoirs which were built in the mid nineteenth century to provide pure water for the people of Liverpool. Neither the seventeenth-century parish church nor the eighteenth-century Unitarian chapel is open to visitors, but the interiors of the two seventeenth-century cruck barns can be seen, because they are now cafes. Lord Leverhulme bought the Rivington estate in 1900 and laid out much of it as Lever Park. The grounds of his own house further up the hill, now called the Rivington Terraced Gardens, can also be visited (see chapter 5).

SILVERDALE
Mrs Gaskell frequently came to Silverdale in the 1850s and stayed with her children at Lindeth Tower for peace and quiet, writing her novels in a room looking over the sands to the hills of Lakeland. Since her day many people have come to Silverdale to retire, but some of the village is as she would remember it. Not so the fine parish church, however, which was built in 1886 in the manner of churches of the fourteenth century, with very spirited carvings on the capitals of its pillars. Silverdale is now a good centre for walks in the Area of Outstanding Natural Beauty (see chapter 2), a beautiful small-scale landscape of limestone rocks and coppiced woodland like Eaves Wood, and also of saltmarshes fringed with low cliffs along which one can walk to Jenny Brown's Point or, in the other direction, around the headland to Arnside.

SLAIDBURN
A place of stone cottages fronted by pebble pavements, Slaidburn is the principal village in the Hodder valley. It is also one of the most attractive in Lancashire, and this is doubtless because, like Downham, it is in the ownership of a single caring landlord. The village is strung out between the cluster of the church (see chapter 4) and the early eighteenth century school at the south end, and the green and bridge at the north, with the Hark to Bounty inn (which used to house the manor court) in the middle. Upstream lies Stocks Reservoir (where one may fish), beyond which the road runs over the lonely fells past the Cross of Greet to Bentham; downstream the

Above: *Pendle Hill from Ribchester.*

Hodder flows past the pretty villages of Newton and Dunsop Bridge before the valley
narrows to a tree-hung gorge at Whitewell,
known locally, and with pardonable exaggera-
tion, as Little Switzerland.

Below: *The White Bull at Ribchester.*

THORNTON CLEVELEYS
Early closing Wednesday.
Thornton Cleveleys is a hybrid, largely
residential town lying between Blackpool and
Fleetwood. To the west Cleveleys is a small
seaside resort with a sandy beach which was
developed between the wars, while to the east
Thornton is more industrial, with a windmill
dated 1794 (see chapter 7) and the vast ICI
chemical plant at Burn Naze, established to
use brine extracted from the sandstone under
the lands on the eastern side of the Wyre.

UPHOLLAND
Upholland is the southernmost town in the
present county and sits on the Ashurst-Billinge
ridge where the old road from Wigan to
Ormskirk rises up in an immense S-bend to
cross it. At the bottom of the hill stands the
church of St Thomas (see chapter 4) and there
are several seventeenth-century houses on the
way up. At the top, beyond the hairpin bend,
one can turn north towards Parbold and drive
to Ashurst Beacon, or follow the main road
westwards towards the new town of **Skelmersdale.** This was designated in 1961 to accommo-

59

Whalley Abbey.

date families from Liverpool and was built during the following twenty years according to a plan which rigorously separates industrial areas from housing estates, and trafficked roads from footpaths between the houses and the town centre.

To the east of the whole town the ground rises steeply to the ridge on which Ashurst Beacon stands and where a golf course and the Beacon Country Park (see chapter 2) provide a fine view across the West Lancashire Plain and over to Liverpool and the hills of Wales.

WARTON

Warton is a long straggling village of limestone cottages, built on the eastern flank of Warton Crag and now greatly extended by suburban estates towards the motorway. Opposite the medieval church, which contains in its tower a stone carved with the arms of the Washington family (the ancestor of the Stars and Stripes), there stand the ruins of Warton Old Rectory, the oldest house in the county (see chapter 3). Warton Crag is more impressive than high, and therefore easy to climb; from the top there are fine views both towards the Lakeland hills and also towards those of the Forest of Bowland.

A couple of miles or so to the north the villages of Yealand Conyers and Yealand Redmayne are strung out on the old main road

which runs along the extended flank of Warton Crag. The villages are linked in name but not in character. Both have seventeenth-century farmhouses and eighteenth-century cottages, but in **Yealand Conyers** the road is winding and hilly, and several big early nineteenth-century houses in their own gardens give it an air of well treed and wealthy suburbia; **Yealand Redmayne,** by contrast, is much more open, with views east over to Ingleborough. The Friends' Meeting House in Yealand Conyers is worth a short visit (see chapter 4). To the west of the hill lies the park of Leighton Hall (see chapter 5) and below that is Leighton Moss (see chapter 2) with its famous bird sanctuary.

WHALLEY
Early closing Wednesday.

One of the most attractive small towns in Lancashire, Whalley has benefited greatly from the construction of the Clitheroe bypass; one can now enjoy the old houses and the view up King Street to Whalley Nab in comparative safety. The town was established where the old road along the southern flank of the Ribble valley crossed the Calder — some of the masonry of the bridge is medieval — and it was for a long time a place of some consequence. Before and after the Norman Conquest it was the centre of an immense parish covering the

60

valleys of the Calder and the Ribble between the Pennine watershed and the Forest of Bowland; the church (see chapter 4) reflects this importance. The old cottages along Church Street are pleasing, and those around The Square form an attractive ensemble with the church and the abbey gateway. The abbey ruins beyond the gatehouse (see chapter 3) are also worth a visit and one should not miss the great railway viaduct (see chapter 7) beyond the other gatehouse.

WHITWORTH

The long climb up from Rochdale to Bacup is emphasised by the rows of houses which line the road and link the villages of Healey, Whitworth and Facit into one long township. Beyond the steeply inclined remains of the now disused railway line, which was opened in 1881, the landscape is littered with spoil heaps of quarry waste, for this is the area where the famous Rossendale flagstones were quarried. The splendid church of St Bartholomew at Whitworth was opened in 1850 and is being restored on a smaller scale after a fire. At Healey the railway viaduct of 1870 remains as

the magnificent man-made centrepiece in a nature trail (see chapter 2) in the deep and wooded valley of the Spodden.

WYCOLLER

The village of Wycoller has been resurrected by the county council's decision to buy it from the water authority and create there the nucleus of a country park, which is the starting point of the Brontë Way leading to Haworth (see chapter 2). Wycoller originated as a medieval cattle farm in a sheltered hollow by a stream, with grazing grounds on the moors above, and gradually developed into a hamlet. In the seventeenth and eighteenth centuries its farmers took up handloom weaving, because their houses stood beside a packhorse trail from Keighley to Colne; a packhorse bridge with a distorted arch is a much photographed feature. When weaving was mechanised, the village declined; the Elizabethan hall, which is supposed to be the original of Fearndean Manor in Charlotte Brontë's *Jane Eyre*, was abandoned and fell into ruins. The ꜱꜱey was then bought to be flooded as a reservoir, but the plan was fortunately never implemented.

Wycoller.

9
Tourist information centres

Tourist information can be obtained from the following information centres. Those marked with an asterisk (*) are recognised by the English Tourist Board. In those marked (B) it is also possible to book accommodation.

Accrington: Gothic House, St James Street, Accrington. Telephone: 0254 33157.
Blackburn: Town Hall, Blackburn. Telephone: 0254 53277. (* B)
County Information Centre, The Boulevard, Blackburn. Telephone: 0254 681120.
Blackpool: 1 Clifton Street, Blackpool. Telephone: 0253 21623. (* B)
Blackpool Hotel and Guest House Association, 87a Coronation Street, Blackpool. Telephone: 0253 21891. (* B)
Blackpool Airport Terminal Buildings, Squire's Gate Lane, Blackpool. Telephone: 0253 43061. (* B)
Burnley: Burnley Mechanics, Manchester Road, Burnley. Telephone: 0282 30055. (* B)
Charnock Richard: Charnock Richard Services, M6 motorway. Telephone: 0257 793773. (* B)
Chorley: Information Desk, Town Hall, Chorley. Telephone: 02572 65611.
Cleveleys: Brighton Avenue, Cleveleys. Telephone: 03914 853378. (*)
Clitheroe: Council Offices, Church Walk, Clitheroe. Telephone: 0200 25566. (* B)
Fleetwood: Marine Hall, Esplanade, Fleetwood. Telephone: 03917 71141. (* B)
Forton: Forton Services, M6 motorway. Telephone: 0524 792181. (* B)
Lancaster: Dalton Square, Lancaster. Telephone: 0524 32878. (* B)
County Information Centre, Bus Station, Lancaster. Telephone: 0524 841656.
Leyland: Civic Centre, West Paddock, Leyland. Telephone: 0772 421491.
Lytham: The Lifeboat Museum, Lytham Green, Lytham. Telephone: 0283 735271.
Morecambe: Marine Road Central, Morecambe. Telephone: 0524 414110. (* B)
Nelson: 19-23 Leeds Road, Nelson. Telephone: 0282 692890. (* B)
County Information Centre, Bus Station, Nelson. Telephone: 0282 65610.
Ormskirk: County Information Centre, Bus Station, Ormskirk. Telephone: 0695 79062. (B)
Town Hall, 52 Derby Street, Ormskirk. Telephone: 0695 77177.
Preston: Guildhall, Lancaster Road, Preston. Telephone: 0772 53731. (* B)
Public Relations Office, County Hall, Preston. Telephone: 0772 263537.
Rawtenstall: 41-5 Kay Street, Rawtenstall. Telephone: 0706 217777. (* B)
St Anne's: The Square, St Anne's. Telephone: 0253 725610.

The picnic site at the Crook o' Lune.

ANCASHIRE

* Country park, nature reserve etc (Ch.2)
⊓ Ancient monument, prehistoric or Roman(Ch.3)
C Ancient monument, medieval Ch.3
+ Church or chapel (Ch.4)
▲ Historic house or garden (Ch.5)
M Museum or art gallery (Ch.6)
I Industrial heritage site (Ch.7)
■ Town or village (Ch.8)
● Other places mentioned

Index